KU-769-387

Contents

page

List of Illustrations   7

ONE The Centuries before Christ   11
Britain an Island—Stonehenge—The Iron Age—Caesar's Attempted
Conquest

TWO The Early Centuries 0 - AD 1000   15
The Roman Occupation—The English Settlements—The Sutton Hoo
Treasure—The Coming of Christianity to the English—The Mercian
Supremacy—The Viking Invasions—King Alfred's Contributions to
Learning—St Dunstan and Monasticism—The Invasion of the Danes
under King Swein

THREE The Eleventh Century   25
The Monarchy—The Formation of the Scottish Kingdom—Supremacy
of the Danish Vikings—The Events of 1066—The Bayeux Tapestry—
The End of Resistance—Domesday Book—Church Reform and Church
Building—The Kingdom and the Duchy

FOUR The Twelfth Century   34
The Monarchy—Anglo-Scottish Relations—The Overseas Possessions of
the Kings of England—Christendom and Islam—Popes, Kings and
Archbishops—The Cistercian Monasteries—Architecture and Illumination

FIVE The Thirteenth Century   42
The Monarchy—Magna Carta and the Papacy—The Beginnings of
Parliament—Edward I and the Affairs of Wales and Scotland—The
Coming of the Friars—Westminster Abbey and Salisbury Cathedral

SIX The Fourteenth Century   52
The Monarchy—The Affairs of Scotland—The Hundred Years' War—
The Peasants' Revolt, 1381—By What Means to Remove a King?—
The Development of English Architecture—Learning and Literature

page

SEVEN   *The Fifteenth Century*   65
   The Monarchy—Rebellion in Wales and Scotland—The End of the
   Hundred Years' War—The Reigns of James I and James II—The Wars of
   the Roses—The Exploration of the Atlantic—Grammar Schools, Printing
   and the Universities—The Final Development of Gothic Architecture

EIGHT   *The Sixteenth Century*   78
   The Monarchy—James IV of Scotland and the Battle of Flodden—The
   Reformation in England—Renaissance and Reformation in Education—
   The Reformation in Scotland—Ocean Trade and Naval Strength—The
   Rise of the English Theatre
   Two tables showing (a) Tudor and Stuart Succession; (b) Stuart and
   Hanoverian Succession

NINE   *The Seventeenth Century*   99
   The Monarchy—The Disunited Kingdom—New Colonies and Trading
   Posts—London before and after Sir Christopher Wren—Science under
   Royal Patronage

TEN   *The Eighteenth Century*   114
   The Monarchy—Wars with France—The Jacobites and the Union of
   the English and Scottish Parliaments—Farmers and Improvers—Fire
   Engines and Oxygen—Communications by Road and Water—Religion
   and Education—The Anti-Slavery Movement

ELEVEN   *The Nineteenth Century*   133
   The Monarchy—Victory over the French—Parliament and Reform—
   Children, Work and Schooling—The Empire, the Army and the Navy

TWELVE   *The Twentieth Century*   150
   The Monarchy—The Royal Family and the Constitution—The Rise of
   the Labour Party—The Great War, 1914-1918—Pre-war Scientists:
   Post-war Achievements—Willingly to School—The Second World War,
   1939-1945—The Enjoyment of Leisure

Index   174

List of Illustrations

	page
Britain an Island (*US Information Services*)	10
Stonehenge (*Patrick Wilcox*)	12
Bronze Shield (*Mansell Collection*)	13
Iron Age Torc (*British Museum*)	14
Head of Hadrian (*British Museum*)	16
Head of Mithras (*Guildhall Museum*)	16
Sutton Hoo Lyre (*British Museum*)	18
Sutton Hoo Gold Buckle (*British Museum*)	18
Lindisfarne Gospel (*British Museum*)	19
10th Century Cross, Iona (*Radio Times Hulton Picture Library*)	20
Offa's Dyke (*Radio Times Hulton Picture Library*)	21
Gokstad Ship (*Mansell Collection*)	22
Bayeux Tapestry (*Radio Times Hulton Picture Library*)	27
Sowing and Threshing (*Mansell Collection*)	29
Domesday Books (*Public Record Office*)	30
Domesday Book Extract (*Public Record Office*)	30
Old Sarum East Gate (*Dept of the Environment*)	31
Durham Cathedral Nave (*From a painting by Anthony Harper*)	32
Richard I's Seal (*John Freeman*)	37
Becket's Crown (*Mansell Collection*)	39
Old Sarum Sculptures (*Dept of the Environment*)	41
Articles of the Barons (*British Museum*)	42
Simon de Montfort's Seal (*British Museum*)	45
Parliament of Edward I (*John Freeman*)	46
Conway Castle (*J. Allan Cash*)	48
Westminster Abbey Chapter House (*Dept of the Environment*)	50
Salisbury Cathedral (*J. Allan Cash*)	51
Arbroath Abbey (*Scottish Dept of the Environment*)	53
Declaration of Arbroath (*John Freeman*)	54
Wine Trade (*Mansell Collection*)	56
Ghent Castle (*Radio Times Hulton Picture Library*)	57
Westminster Hall (*Author's Collection*)	61
New College, Oxford (*John Freeman*)	62
Page from Wyclif's Bible (*British Museum*)	63

	page
Extract from Caxton's *Dictes* (*British Museum*)	64
Richard, Duke of Warwick, and Henry VI (*British Museum*)	70
King's College, Cambridge (*Author's Collection*)	71
Eton College (*Radio Times Hulton Picture Library*)	74
Divinity School, Oxford (*Thomas Photos*)	75
Boston Stump (*Author's Collection*)	77
Henry VII's Chapel (*British Travel Association*)	77
Page from Tyndale's Bible (*British Museum*)	80
Tintern Abbey (*Dept of the Environment*)	82
Glasgow Cathedral (*Radio Times Hulton Picture Library*)	88
John Knox's House (*Radio Times Hulton Picture Library*)	90
Walmer Castle, Kent (*Dept of the Environment*)	92
Hondius Map of Drake's Voyage (*British Museum*)	93
The Lyte Jewel (*British Museum*)	100
Torn Journal of the House of Commons (*The House of Lords*)	100
Warrant Issued by Charles I (*British Museum*)	102
Seal of the Commonwealth, 1651 (*British Museum*)	104
Tobacco Pipe and Gold Ring (*Author's Collection*)	107
Exchequer Bills, 1696, 1697, 1709 (*Bank of England*)	108
Tilbury Fort (*Dept of the Environment*)	109
Wren's Plan for St Paul's (*Mansell Collection*)	111
Boyle's Air Pump (*Author's Collection*)	113
Treaty of Paris (*Public Record Office*)	117
Parliamentary Union: Pamphlets (*British Museum*)	118
Glenfinnan (*British Travel Association*)	120
Chiswick House (*Dept of the Environment*)	122
Chiswick House Portico (*Dept of the Environment*)	122
Saxtead Green Post Mill (*Dept of the Environment*)	123
Quotation from Swift (*Derek Benney*)	124
Newcomen's Fire Engine (*Science Museum*)	125
Watt's Rotary Steam Engine (*Science Museum*)	126
John Wesley (*Methodist Missionary Society*)	130
Lord Cochrane's Recruiting Poster (*National Maritime Museum*)	134
Penmaen Mawr Railway Line (*Samuel Smiles*)	138
Tube for the Britannia Bridge (*Samuel Smiles*)	139
St Dunstan's College (*Leslie Morris*)	144
Sokol, First Ship to Exceed 30 Knots (*Grace Crush*)	145
Winston Churchill, aged 24 (*Lady Churchill*)	149
The House of Commons (*Radio Times Hulton Picture Library*)	152
Avro 504 (*Science Museum*)	155
Field Gun at Zillebeke (*Imperial War Museum*)	158

	page
Mark V Tank (*Imperial War Museum*)	159
Fleming's Valve (*Science Museum*)	160
Einstein's Blackboard (*History of Science Museum, Oxford*)	161
Vapour Trails round St Paul's (*Radio Times Hulton Picture Library*)	166
Battalion Orders 1944 (*Regimental Headquarters, Winchester*)	169
View from a Cottage Garden, Selworthy, Sussex (*British Travel Association*)	173

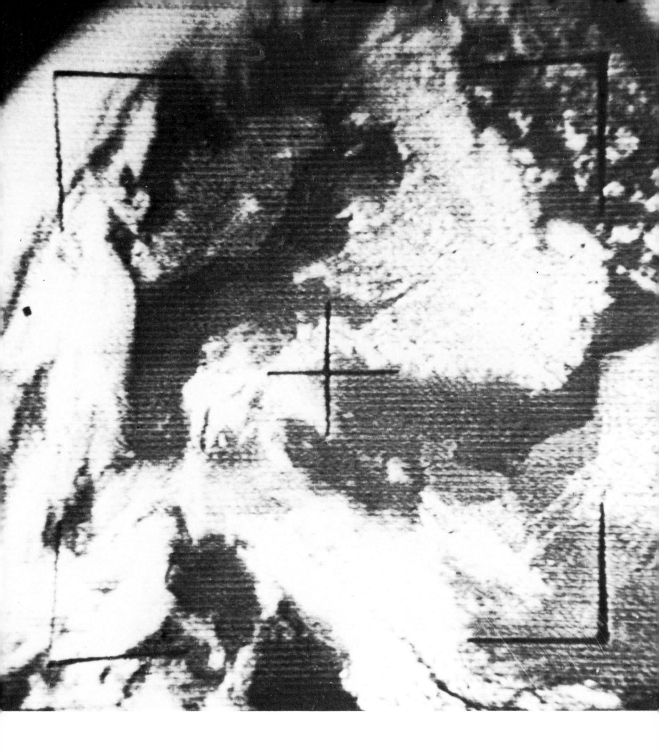

Britain an Island. From outer space the television camera of a US satellite reveals through a rift in Atlantic storm clouds the shape of the British Isles with the exactness of a map such as seamen have longed for through the centuries

CHAPTER ONE

The Centuries Before Christ

Britain an Island

Britain did not become an island until after the last Ice Age; then, about 6000 BC, ocean tides tore a way through the chalky hills which once lay between Dover and Calais and flooded the plain that now lies below the North Sea. This left an island divided into two zones; the mountainous west and north, where all the year round cold hills suck the rain from Atlantic storms; and the lowland east and south, where grassy downlands thrust up through the forests and fens, tempting invaders from the continent with milder weather and lighter soils.

Until about 2000 BC the inhabitants of Britain were Stone Age hunters and fishers, finding abundant food along the coast and in the rivers, woods and marshes. Then from across the North Sea men of a more civilised race, able to manufacture bronze, colonised the chalk downs and limestone plateaux of the east and south. In their graves are found decorated pots of beaker shape and from these they have been named the Beaker people.

On Salisbury Plain the Beaker people mingled with another highly gifted race coming from the western coasts, which they seem to have reached from the direction of Spain and Brittany. They left long barrows, hollow cairns and dolmens which can be seen in profusion in Ireland, on headlands along the north coast of Cornwall, and in the west of Wales. In Scotland such monuments are found in the west and extreme north-east. Stonehenge is their supreme achievement.

Stonehenge

Stonehenge is in effect an astronomical clock 100 feet in diameter, its huge monolithic columns having been erected in two concentric rings so that the sun's disc can be seen framed exactly between two of them as it rises above the horizon at the winter solstice. Though erected about 1500 BC, sixteen out of the original thirty uprights still stand and several support stone lintels fixed with mortice joints across their tops. The builders chose seventy-five irregularly shaped sandstone boulders or sarsens from those left on the top of Marlborough downs when the rain of centuries had washed away the softer soils in which they were once embedded. These sarsens they shaped into rectangular blocks, the tallest of which is 22 feet high and is sunk a further 8 feet into the ground. The transport and erection of such a heavy monolith required immense effort. In

addition, bluestones weighing up to 4½ tons form an inner ring. A possible clue to the origin of the builders was found in 1953, when numerous axe head signs of a kind known to have been used by an axe cult in ancient Greece were discovered on the base of some of the monoliths.

The Iron Age

About 500 BC the inhabitants of Britain began to learn how to manufacture iron, though the tin required for bronze-founding in the Mediterranean area continued to

*Bronze shield of about 100 BC, found
in the Thames near Battersea in 1857.
The embossed design is enhanced with
studs of red enamel*

be a valuable export from Cornwall. It is from the Mediterranean that the first written account of the islanders has come down. Pytheas of Massilia (now Marseilles), a scholar and traveller who circumnavigated Britain about 310 BC, said that it was triangular in shape; that to the west lay another large island and five days' sail to the north of Scotland an island called Thule (possibly Iceland). He called the inhabitants Celts, and described them as skilled wheat farmers, usually peaceable, but formidable in war, when they used horse-drawn chariots (as Julius Caesar was to learn 250 years later).

The last of the Iron Age invasions occurred in 75 BC, and resulted in the setting-up of a Celtic kingdom astride the Channel. Of this Caesar learned in 55 BC, when he was preparing his first expedition. After his swift conquest of Gaul in the previous three years, he realised that refugees in Britain might stir up a rebellion on the continent, and so he decided on a sudden blow against them.

13

Caesar's Attempted Conquest

Caesar did not leave Gaul till late in the summer of 55 BC, sailing at midnight and arriving off the cliffs of Dover on 25th August. With him were the Seventh and Tenth Legions, about 10,000 men; the cavalry were to follow. Their approach had been betrayed and an army was ready to oppose a landing. After fierce fighting the Romans got ashore near Deal; the enemy offered to submit and surrender hostages. During the negotiations a storm battered the Roman fleet and drove the cavalry transports back to Gaul. Caesar, anticipating that the enemy would take advantage of these misfortunes to renew their attacks, laid a successful trap and again drove them off. In spite of this victory, however, he decided to take his army back to Gaul before autumn gales began.

The following May he assembled a force twice as large as before and this time landed near Deal unopposed, but he had not advanced far inland before a storm destroyed forty of his ships and damaged many more. While repairs were put in hand, the Romans marched towards London, harassed by an enemy for the most part hidden in the woods. Caesar recorded: 'The Britons call it a fort when they defend a tract of dense forest with a rampart and a ditch.' After a victory in Hertfordshire news of an impending rebellion in Gaul caused the Romans to withdraw once again.

Twice Caesar's career had come near to ruin on the coast of Kent. He had taken great risks, as all empire-builders must, but even in defeat he planted in the imagination of his countrymen the ambition to rule Britain and so command her mines of tin, lead and silver and her exports of wheat. Some Romans jeered, as Cicero did in writing to a friend: 'It is now known for certain that there is not one pennyweight of silver in the whole island, and no hope of plunder except in the form of slaves.' Others went on to found an empire that at the height of its power stretched from the Highlands of Scotland to the Persian Gulf.

A torc, or bracelet, belonging to the 1st century BC. Found at Snettisham in Norfolk with other treasure; made of electrum, a pale alloy of silver and gold

CHAPTER TWO

The Early Centuries, 0-AD 1000

The Roman Occupation

The century following Caesar's expeditions was one of prosperity for Britain, not of peace. In spite of tribal wars towns flourished in the east and south, notably at or near the sites of Colchester, St Albans, Silchester and Winchester. The king who reigned at Colchester, Cunobelinus, issued gold coins bearing an ear of wheat, the source of his wealth; it was his death which gave the Romans a fresh opportunity for conquest. In AD 43 they assembled a force of 20,000 and landed unopposed at Richborough in Kent, where a safe land-locked harbour had formed since Caesar's time.

The Romans followed Caesar's line of march towards London. After a battle the crossing of the Medway was won and Colchester captured. From there the legions fought their way west into Dorset and north-west to the Severn, where for years they were harassed by Caractacus, son of Cunobelinus, who did not fall into their hands until AD 50. Then he was paraded in triumph through the streets of Rome, where his proud bearing won him unusual clemency—pardon and freedom from the Emperor Claudius, who had himself been present at the capture of Colchester.

In Britain the spoils of victory were already being taken with oppressive greed. A cruel state monopoly exploited British minerals, especially the silver-bearing lead mines of the Mendips. In the east traders and money-lenders provoked a terrible revolt, that of Boudicca, a native queen who in AD 61 ravaged and burnt Colchester and London. Peace and prosperity were not restored until the wise administration of the Roman general Agricola (AD 78-83). In AD 83 he defeated the clans of Caledonia, possibly near Perth.

The Emperor Hadrian, after a revolt in the north, inspected the frontier in AD 122, and ordered a wall and a ditch to be built along the 70 miles between the mouth of the Tyne and Solway Firth. For 40 miles the eastern part was in stone 10 feet thick and 20 feet high, with watch towers and forts at regular intervals, and the western end was completed with an earthwork 20 feet thick at the base.

Hadrian's wall did not mark the limit of Roman power. Inchtuthill on the river Tay was the most northerly of their fortresses. In AD 142 after another revolt a barrier was built between the Firth of Forth and the Firth of Clyde; this was of turf 15 feet thick at the base and 37 miles long, but in AD 180 it had to be evacuated. Even Hadrian's wall

(left) The Emperor Hadrian (reigned AD 117-138). A bronze head found in the river Thames at London Bridge; (right) Mithras, god of soldiers and merchants. A marble head found in 1954 among the ruins of his temple in the city of London. The Mithras cult demanded of its devotees courage, the soldier's virtue, and honesty, the merchant's

was twice overrun and twice repaired—under the Emperor Severus, who died at York in AD 211, and under Constantius, father of the Emperor Constantine, who was given command in Britain in AD 296. It was finally overrun about AD 385.

Though Roman domination north of the Tyne and west of the Severn was often insecure, life in the south and east reached a standard of ordered peace and civilisation not subsequently attained until Tudor times. The leading families among the subject population imitated the Roman way of life, living in great farmhouses far from town, visiting such urban attractions as the hot springs at Bath, the amphitheatre at Chester or the temple of Mithras in London, and enjoying luxury goods imported from Europe.

After AD 200 more unsettled times began. Towns previously unwalled were fortified and castles built near the shore as bases for naval operations against invaders from Germany. Not until AD 476 did the Roman empire in the west finally collapse, but for a century before that conditions in Britain had become typical of the Middle Ages and life was 'nasty, brutish and short.'

With Christianity, however, the British isles inherited from the Roman empire a sense of unity and an ideal of peace which survived every disaster. Three bishops from Britain were delegates to the Church Council held at Arles in AD 314, a sign that the truth of the Gospel had triumphed over Celtic superstition, to which the Romans showed only the easy tolerance of non-belief, having lost all faith in their own gods. Nor did Christian missionaries stop at the boundaries of the empire; they penetrated Scotland and Ireland, laying the foundations on which civilised life could be recreated after the barbarian invasions.

The English Settlements

Between AD 400 and 600 yet another invasion of Britain from across the North Sea achieved more lasting effects than any other. The invaders brought with them the basis of a language both eloquent and flexible that has since become the lingua franca of half the world. Their skill in agriculture and forestry enabled them to conquer the midland forests which the Celts had eschewed. Today the names of countless hamlets are proof of the thoroughness with which they colonised; and great cities like Birmingham and Nottingham, called after two chieftains now forgotten, testify to the wisdom with which they chose sites for their settlements.

For purposes of local government they gradually divided the island into counties and shires—Norfolk to the north folk, Suffolk to the south, and so on—choosing geographical boundaries so sensibly that before the Norman conquest the English system of taxation was more efficient than any other in Europe, and the same county divisions that were then appropriate for a population of less than two million are still proudly maintained by fifty million today.

Yet nothing but the barest outline of how and by what stages this extraordinary transformation was achieved can be reconstructed from the literary sources or archeological discoveries so far made. In later centuries chroniclers and story-writers recorded (with embellishments) what they had learned from oral tradition about the two centuries during which the English nation was born, but this is difficult to interpret. The King Arthur of medieval romance may in fact have been some temporarily successful general, but no date or place can be given for the victories he is reputed to have won over the pagan invaders. It is their gods and goddesses, Woden, Thor and Frig, who are remembered in the names of the days of the week, and only after the age of settlement were their descendants gradually weaned from the warlike divinities of Valhalla who seemed to come with such powerful aid to their worshippers on earth.

According to Bede, the monk of Jarrow whose history of the English church was completed in 731, the invaders consisted of Angles from Schleswig, Saxons from north-west Germany, and Jutes from Jutland. The Angles colonised East Anglia; the Saxons, Essex, Sussex and Wessex; and the Jutes, Kent and the Isle of Wight. Though an excellent historian, Bede was writing long after the event and evidence now available shows that the Frisian islanders and the whole population from Jutland south to Holland was involved in the migration, making it impossible to be so precise as Bede about the movements of people who, acting in small independent groups, sought their fortunes in a hostile land. The process of immigration must in fact have been slow and cautious. First this piece of coastline would be probed, then that; one year this river would be explored, in another that forest would be pierced. In some places the whole Romano-Celtic population may have been killed or forced into exile; in many others they were probably enslaved and forced to work for the newcomers.

The Sutton Hoo Treasure

The haphazard nature of archeological evidence could not be better illustrated than by the almost revolutionary change in historical thinking caused by the discovery at Sutton Hoo in 1939 of a collection of splendid arms and armour, eating utensils, and personal jewellery fashioned in gold, silver and enamel work by highly skilled craftsmen of native and foreign birth, together with gold coin from eastern France.

About 650 this treasure, intended for the use of some chieftain in the next world, had been ceremonially buried in a large rowing boat that had been dragged to the top

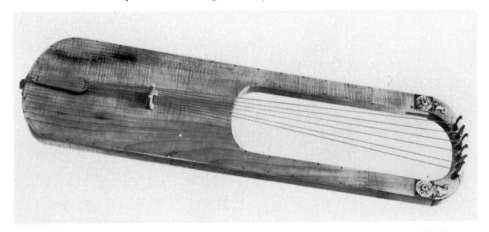

(above) Lyre reconstructed from the remains found at Sutton Hoo in 1939. It is nearly 30 inches long; (below) Gold buckle with niello inlay found at Sutton Hoo in 1939. It is of English craftsmanship and made in two linked parts. At the tip is a carving of a dog chasing its own paw

18

of a low promontory (*hoo*) on a Suffolk river estuary. When this barrow was opened it was found that the gentle pressure of the sand had retained the imprint of the boat's timbers and had crushed, but not destroyed, the contents of the treasure house amidships. No trace, however, has been found of the chieftain's body; previously people of such wealth had been thought to belong only to Kent, but the presence of Swedish work among the jewellery suggests that the invaders may have come from further afield and been more highly civilised than hitherto supposed.

The Coming of Christianity to the English

It is possible that the chieftain commemorated at Sutton Hoo was the Christian ruler of a pagan people and that his body was given Christian burial elsewhere. He lived at a time of change when this could have happened. In 597 Pope Gregory the Great had sent a company of monks led by Augustine to Canterbury, the capital of a pagan king named Ethelbert who had married a Christian princess from Paris. So rapidly did Christ's doctrine take root that Ethelbert was baptised and endowed the Church with land. Augustine was made a bishop and given instructions for the conversion of the whole island. In 601 Pope Gregory wrote to him: 'You know, my brother, the custom of the Roman Church, but my advice is that you should make a careful selection of anything that you have found either in the Roman or the Gallic, or any other Church which may be more acceptable to Almighty God and diligently teach the Church of

The opening words of St John's Gospel in the Latin manuscript written and illuminated on Holy Island (Lindisfarne)

19

A 10th century cross on the island of Iona, Scotland

the English. Choose therefore from each Church those things that are pious, religious, and seemly and when you have, as it were, incorporated them, let the minds of the English be accustomed to them.'

The Gospel reached the north, however, from a different source. Christianity had survived from Roman times in Ireland and south-west Scotland and was kept alive by monks who were not, like the Benedictines, cloistered, but moved freely among the people. Nor did they set up an organisation by parishes and dioceses as in the Roman church. Missionaries from the monastery on Iona, founded about 563 by Columba, reached many parts of Scotland and in 635 were asked to come to the court of Oswald, King of Northumbria, who had lived in Scotland before his accession. Those sent were headed by Aidan, a most gifted man, who made his headquarters on Lindisfarne (also called Holy Island) off the Northumbrian coast.

The converts of this northern Celtic church were persuaded to adopt Roman customs at the Synod of Whitby in 663 by a Greek scholar-statesman, Theodore of Tarsus, whom the Pope had appointed Archbishop of Canterbury. To strengthen the northern churches Theodore chose Cuthbert, a man renowned for his saintly life, as Bishop of Lindisfarne, and there, about 700, an artist-monk named Eadfrith made an illuminated manuscript copy of the Gospels, now one of the chief glories of the British Museum.

20

Its pictures reflect an English love of birds, beasts and fishes which still draws men to the island.

In the eighth century the English church became the most influential in northern Europe. A Devon man, Boniface, worked as a missionary among the Frisians and was made Archbishop of Mainz. Alcuin, a scholar-poet from York, became the Emperor Charlemagne's chief adviser on educational matters.

The Mercian Supremacy

Between 700 and 800 the kings of Mercia, whose territory reached across the Midlands from the borders of Wales to the North Sea, made themselves supreme over a much wider area, including Kent, Surrey and Sussex, and claimed to be overlords of the kings of Wessex and Northumbria. Their names were Ethelbald (716-757) and Offa (757-796). The power of Offa is exemplified in two ways; he engineered a rampart-barrier, or dyke, along seventy miles of his western border to assist its defence against Welsh inroads; and he set up mints that issued the first coinage to be common currency throughout Britain since Roman times. One magnificent gold coin of his minting, called a dinar, became currency among traders dealing with the countries conquered in the previous century by the Arab followers of Mahomet. He also corresponded with the Pope and renewed the bonds between the English Church and the continent.

Part of Offa's Dyke in Denbighshire. An earthwork, its height has been much reduced by 1,200 years of frost, snow and rain

The Viking Invasions

Offa and his contemporary Charlemagne, King of the Franks, the founder of the Holy Roman Empire, seemed to create a prospect of ordered progress in Europe. Then in 845 a force of pagan warriors from Scandinavia entered the Seine. This was in the dominions of Charles the Bald, a grandson of Charlemagne, a scholar not a general, who failed to organise any resistance; the people of Paris fled, leaving their city and the Seine valley to be plundered. It was an event that horrified Europe. These sea-robbers were the Vikings, a race of men with ships faster and more seaworthy than any previously built and inspired by a religion that taught them to glory in the art of war and the treacheries of diplomacy. In return for a worthless promise to go and not return, they extracted from the Franks 7,000 pounds-weight of silver. It was the first of many Danegelds and bought the Franks little respite.

Before the capture of Paris other Viking forces had attacked the coasts of the British Isles but seldom stayed. In 865, however, a great army from Denmark settled in East

A Viking ship, which lay buried for over 1,000 years under peat moss at Gokstad in southern Norway. Her keel was 60 feet long and the bulwarks rose only 3½ feet above it. Amidships, where she was 15½ feet broad, the strong seating for the single mast can be clearly seen. With a broad lug sail and sixteen oars on either side, such ships could travel fast and gave the Vikings supremacy in the 9th century

Anglia, raiding places as far inland as Reading. In 866 they stormed York and the next year destroyed the Northumbrian army.

Four years later a Viking army from East Anglia suddenly, in mid-winter, attacked Wessex, making a fortified camp at Reading in the angle between the Kennet and the Thames to serve them as a base. In a pitched battle with the men of Wessex on the Berkshire downs they were defeated and forced back to their camp. One of the victors was Alfred, a royal prince of twenty-one, who was made King of Wessex the next year. Other Viking armies already held the rest of England and a long war for Wessex began. In 878 Alfred lured the Vikings under King Guthrum into the woods and marshes of Somerset, and, gathering a much superior force, defeated them near Warminster. They fled to Chippenham and there were allowed to surrender. In Viking fashion they promised everything to get away. Guthrum and other leaders consented to be baptised and in future to observe the line of Watling Street, the old Roman road from London to Chester, as the boundary between Wessex and the Danelaw, as the Viking-dominated part of the country was called. This treaty of Wedmore was, unexpectedly, observed for seven years.

When war was renewed, Alfred captured London and then attacked the Vikings in Essex. During the peace he had imported Dutchmen to build and man warships exceeding in length, and therefore in the number of oars, those which had previously given the Vikings supremacy, and it was this fleet which brought Alfred victory in Essex, and enabled him to repel attacks along the south coast. He showed subsequent generations that the men from the north had no monopoly of shipbuilding or seamanship and were not invincible either on sea or land.

King Alfred's Contributions to Learning

As a boy Alfred had been sent to Rome to be educated, and became a godson of the Pope. His youth was spent fighting the Vikings, and when peace came, he acquired a command of Latin which enabled him to supervise and assist in a translation of Pope Gregory's *Pastoral Care*, which he distributed to churchmen for their guidance. To a translation of a history of the world he added an account of a voyage along the Norwegian coast from above the Arctic circle, and to a book of Latin philosophy many homely Anglo-Saxon similes. For this work he attracted to his court at Winchester scholars from other parts of England and from the continent.

As a lawgiver he relied on earlier edicts, but added new provisions to replace by royal justice such ancient customs as the blood-feud. The compilation of the *Anglo-Saxon Chronicle* was also begun under his direction; it could not throw much light on earlier centuries, but was subsequently kept up as a summary of current affairs and became an invaluable authority on such events as the Norman Conquest, on which it differs significantly from Norman writers.

St Dunstan and Monasticism

The destruction by the Vikings of the monasteries of Northumbria and East Anglia left the church north of the Thames very weak. The original ideals of monasticism had everywhere been forgotten until enthusiasm for the Benedictine Rule was revived by Dunstan, a monk of Glastonbury in Somerset. In the course of a long and saintly life (909-988) he became Archbishop of Canterbury and the chief adviser of King Edgar, who reigned from 959 to 975 and at whose command the monasteries at Ely and Peterborough were richly re-endowed.

The Invasion of the Danes under King Swein

For seventy years after the death of Alfred in 901 the gradual acceptance of Christianity by the Vikings who settled in the Danelaw went on and English kings of the royal house of Wessex endeavoured by various means to reassert their authority in the north. Communications were, however, too slow and variations in speech and customary law between north and south too sharp for any real unification to be achieved; only peaceful coexistence proved possible.

From 988 onwards, political upheavals in Scandinavia led to renewed and very powerful attacks by Vikings from Denmark and Norway, particularly in the west. Then in 994 Swein Forkbeard, King of Denmark, accompanied by the Norwegian Olaf Tryggvason, arrived in the Thames with a fleet of 100 ships and about 2,000 men. The Londoners repulsed them, but they plundered south-east England until bought off with 16,000 pounds-weight of silver. Olaf did not return, but Viking raids continued throughout the 990s. In churches everywhere the prayer went up: 'From the fury of the Northmen, good Lord, deliver us!'

The power of the Vikings, based on their command of the sea, made defence against surprise attacks most difficult; with their ships, now much improved in design and speed, they could move rapidly, often at night; and on land, being natural horsemen, they stole mounts that could carry them still more swiftly to their prey. Danegeld, which the English were forced to pay by way of taxation, was one form of defence, and it had the effect of greatly widening the gap between the rich and poor. The first settlers had been free soldier-craftsmen, independent and even impatient of army life, but by the end of the tenth century feudal levies, recruited for local defence, had become touchingly devoted to their lords. In the *Song of Maldon*, celebrating a fight with the Vikings in Essex in 991, one of Earl Brithnorth's men says: '*Thoughts must be braver, hearts more valiant, courage the greater as strength grows less. Here lies our lord, all cut down, the hero in the dust. I will not leave the field, but think to lie by my lord's side, by the man I hold so dear.*'

24

CHAPTER THREE

The Eleventh Century

The Monarchy

England		Scotland	
*Ethelred II	979–1013	Kenneth III	997–1005
Swein Forkbeard	1013–1014	Malcolm II	1005–1034
*Ethelred II	1014–1016	Duncan I	1034–1040
Edmund Ironside	1016	Macbeth	1040–1057
Canute the Dane	1017–1035	Malcolm III	1058–1093
Harold I	1035–1040	*Donald Ban	1093
Hardicanute	1040–1042	Duncan II	1094
Edward the Confessor	1042–1066	*Donald Ban	1094–1097
Harold II	1066	Edgar	1097–1107
William I	1066–1087		
William II Rufus	1087–1100		

*Deposed and then restored

The Formation of the Scottish Kingdom

Until the tenth century chroniclers used the Latin word Scotia as a name for Ireland; then it began to be used as the name for that part of modern Scotland which lies north of the Forth and Clyde, and the Forth was sometimes called 'the Scots Water.' It was only after the Norman conquest of England that Scotia was used to include the whole of modern Scotland, and for some centuries the Scottish kingdom was spoken of as having three parts, Galloway, Lothian and, north of the Forth and Clyde, Scotland.

The Roman rulers of Britain regarded the inhabitants of the Highlands, whom they called Caledonians or Picts, as enemies and suffered many defeats from them. The Scots, who came over the narrow waters from Ireland to help the Picts, had by 500 established a dominion astride the sea, part in Argyll and part in Ireland, and by 574 Columba, the missionary who carried the Gospel from Ireland to Scotland, had made Aidan ruler of this sea kingdom.

In 603 Aidan and the Scots met an army from the English settlements in Lothian and were defeated. To this English pressure from the south-east was added, from about 840, pressure from the Vikings on the islands and coasts of the north and west, where they raided and plundered for thirty years and then settled in large numbers. This forced the Picts and Scots to combine and in 843 they recognised Kenneth MacAlpin as king.

Malcolm II's defeat of an English army from Northumbria at Carham on the Tweed in 1018 left his successor, Duncan I, supreme over the land now called Scotland with the exception of Orkney, Shetland, the Western Isles and large tracts on the mainland in the north still held by the Vikings.

The extraordinary mixture of races over which the kings of Scotland ruled may be judged from their habit even in the twelfth century of addressing them in this order: French (meaning the recent Anglo-Norman invaders); English (those who had settled in Lothian); Scots; Welsh (meaning the people in the Dumbarton area whose ancestors had settled there after being driven out of Britain when Roman power failed); and lastly the people of Galloway.

Supremacy of the Danish Vikings

In the autumn of 1002 King Ethelred of England, called the Unready (meaning Redeless, that is 'without good counsel') planned the greatest crime of his long reign. It had been a bad year for Viking raids; 24,000 pounds of silver had been paid in Danegeld, and on 13 November a great massacre of Vikings south of the Danelaw took place on the king's command. The sister of Swein Forkbeard, King of Denmark, was among those murdered. Swein, after organising a long series of raids, judged that the people of the Danelaw would support him if he led an attempt to conquer the whole land. In 1013, after Swein had penetrated the Thames valley and captured Bath, Ethelred fled to the court of Duke Richard of Normandy, whose sister he had married as his second wife. Swein, now acknowledged ruler of all England, did not live to enjoy his triumph, but died suddenly in February 1014. His young son Canute withdrew his army to Denmark, but returned in 1017 and reigned successfully for eighteen years. He did not treat England as a colony, but he was regarded as a foreigner. His dominions included at one time Norway, Denmark, and part of Scotland as well as England, but this empire did not last. The sons who succeeded him died in quick succession, and in 1042 Ethelred's son Edward, later named the Confessor, returned from exile in Normandy to be made king.

The Events of 1066

On 5 January 1066, after a long illness, Edward the Confessor died, childless, and the English people expected, and greatly feared, a war for the throne. There were four contestants: Harold Godwin, the richest landowner in southern England, who had himself crowned king immediately; William, Duke of Normandy, the Confessor's nearest male relative, who, though a bastard, had inherited the duchy and made himself the most powerful prince in Europe; a brother of Harold Godwin named Tostig, whom the Confessor had exiled; and Harold Hardrada, a general famous for his victories in the East and now King of Norway.

Fears for the future increased when in April a great comet appeared in the heavens, blazing by night and day. In May Tostig raided the south coast, but was driven off.

He then joined forces with the King of Norway and in September their fleet of 300 ships came to land unopposed near York, and defeated the local forces sent against them. King Harold marched north at once, and, taking the Vikings by surprise, overwhelmed them at Stamford Bridge on 25 September. Harold Hardrada and Tostig were killed in action, and only thirty of their ships were needed to take home those whom the English king spared. Three days later Duke William landed at Pevensey in Sussex.

King Harold moved south without delay, calling on all available forces to meet him near Hastings, but there, on 14 October, he was forced to fight a defensive battle. He and two of his brothers were killed and his whole force routed. At one stroke Duke William had won a kingdom. His good fortune had been immense; he had crossed the channel very late in the year, and might have had to fight a long winter campaign. Cautiously he marched towards London. In him and his companions in arms the passion for overseas conquest, inherited from their Viking ancestors, who had colonised the Seine valley a century before, was tempered by statecraft and a desire to have the blessing of the Church on their ambitions.

On Christmas Day 1066, he was crowned by the English Archbishop of Canterbury in the vast Norman-style abbey church built by Edward the Confessor at Westminster. The archbishop asked the congregation in English whether they accepted William as king; and the same question was asked in French by the Bishop of Coutances. There were shouts of assent. On the same spot the reigning archbishop has crowned all subsequent monarchs of England.

A scene from the Bayeux Tapestry. A group of courtiers are astounded by the appearance of a large comet flying over the palace of King Harold at Westminster. The artist tells a continuous story in pictures, and in the next scene he shows a messenger telling the king this dreadful news. Below the ghostly outline of ships presages the invasion. The Latin words are: Isti mirant stellam. *The movement of the comet, which appears at roughly 75-year intervals, was first predicted by Edmund Halley, a friend of Sir Isaac Newton*

The Bayeux Tapestry

The English were famous all over Europe for their skill in embroidery—it was called the English art—and no example of it is more remarkable than the Bayeux Tapestry in which pictures telling the story of 1066 are embroidered in coloured wools on a strip of linen over 200 feet long. It was probably done about twenty years after the event for the Conqueror's half-brother, Odo of Bayeux, Bishop of Rochester, and the artist follows the account of Harold's conduct given in Norman documents, not in the *Anglo-Saxon Chronicle*.

The End of Resistance

The tall, burly figure of the new king, backed by a strong show of force, was enough to command obedience from the English in most places, but not in the north. Early in 1069 a Norman earl was burned alive in the bishop's house at Durham. Later that year Swein Estrithson, King of Norway, brought 240 Viking ships into the Humber. The men of the north joined him and massacred the Norman garrison in York. King William took a swift and terrible revenge, devastating Yorkshire and bribing the Danes to depart. They returned the next year, led by the King of Denmark, and helped Hereward the Wake to loot the abbey of Peterborough, but left again, content with plunder only.

Further north the King of Scotland, Malcolm III, who had married Margaret, an English princess, laid waste the Durham countryside. William, in retaliation, undertook the most daring of all his campaigns. In 1072, marching up the east coast with a fleet in close attendance, he crossed the Forth and reached the Tay. Without a battle Malcolm sued for peace, recognised William as his overlord, and surrendered hostages. The whole kingdom was at last secure in Norman hands.

The remaining fifteen years of William's reign were comparatively peaceful, but in 1087, in one of many quarrels with the King of France, William burnt Mantes and in a riding accident there received injuries from which he died.

Domesday Book

From 1066 the king benefited from the excellent system of taxation evolved for the payment of Danegeld and from a monetary system in which a large number of local mints were controlled by the central government in Winchester, but in 1086 no one knew the economic strength of the kingdom after twenty years of peaceful change. Following a conference to which the king called all the chief men of the realm, royal commissioners visited most of the shires and counties and wrote down the number of freemen, farmers and serfs living in each locality; the number of ploughs, horses, fields, woods, fisheries and saltpans each village possessed; and many other details, including a comparison of 1066 with 1086 values. Such precise information over so vast an area had never been collected by any other ruler; the enterprise astounded the Conqueror's contemporaries, who felt that it put him in a position not unlike that of God on Judgement Day (Domesday). The original Latin manuscript summarising the commissioners' findings is at the Public Record Office; it is a masterpiece of tabulation, and no other medieval document of equal age gives so complete a picture of economic life at the time it was compiled. With it as reference, the Exchequer officials could, whenever a feudal due came up for payment, fix a sum proportionate to the wealth of the person or corporate body concerned. Out of 180 great landowners whose possessions were listed only six were Englishmen, so completely had the wealth of the country been taken over by the conquerors, a small French-speaking minority in an English population estimated at between one and two million.

Two scenes from an 11th century calendar showing (a) digging and sowing in March, and (b) threshing and winnowing in December. The man digging is wielding a mattock above his head, another, holding the seed in his waist cloth, scatters it broadcast. The impressionist technique for showing clouds racing along in a March wind is typical of Saxon MSS. The winter task of threshing wheat with flails and winnowing the grain with a circular fan is painted with equal vigour

(above) The two volumes of Domesday Book (1086) lying on the iron-bound chest with three locks in which it was traditionally kept at Winchester, the seat of government in Norman times. The second smaller volume contains the returns for Norfolk, Suffolk and Essex, prosperous counties, where there was a great weight of information to collect; (below) The Westminster Abbey Entry in Domesday Book. The Latin begins Terra Sancti Petri, *the land of St Peter, the saint to whom the abbey was dedicated. Four lines from the bottom the letters* TRE *stand for* Tempore Regis Edwardi, *in the time of Edward the Confessor, that is 1065*

Church Reform and Church Building

The Norman conquest brought the Church in England under the powerful influence of foreign bishops and architects. In 1070 the Conqueror appointed as Archbishop of Canterbury, and therefore as one of his chief advisers, Lanfranc, an Italian scholar who had won European fame as a teacher at Le Bec, a Benedictine monastery in Normandy. At this time a celibate priesthood was the aim of the Papacy and the ideal life for a religious man was declared to be that of the monk with his vows of poverty, chastity and obedience and seclusion from the world. For the monks of Canterbury Lanfranc drew up a set of rules, and sent three monks to Scotland to help the saintly Queen Margaret to reform the Church there.

Lanfranc died in 1089 and Rufus, who openly scoffed at religion, kept the valuable revenues of the archbishopric for his own use for four years (other less irreligious kings did likewise when bishoprics fell vacant). At the end of this time Rufus, having fallen ill and being in fear of death, appointed as archbishop Anselm, an Italian of noble birth

The view from the east gate of Old Sarum near Salisbury, Wiltshire. On 1 August 1086 all the more important landowners were commanded to assemble here and do homage to William the Conqueror for their lands, a sign that they owed allegiance not merely to their immediate lords but to him. On this hill top the Normans built a castle and a cathedral within the earth ramparts of an Iron Age fort, which can be seen in the middle distance

The 11th century nave of Durham Cathedral, a building unique in Europe, from a picture painted in 1958 by Anthony Harper, the artist who also executed the stained glass figure of St Cuthbert in one of the windows. The vigorous designs carved on the columns are typical of the best English Romanesque work

32

who had been a pupil of Lanfranc at Le Bec and later become the foremost theologian in Europe. This was done almost by force, as Anselm, hitherto a contemplative scholar, was most unwilling to accept office. When the king recovered, he regretted the appointment and sought to depose him. Anselm, who had not received from the Pope the pallium, a white band symbolic of his office, asked leave to go to Rome, and, being refused, left the country without it. In Rome he was received with honour, but not given the support he asked for; he was still abroad when Rufus was killed.

The increasing power of the bishops in Church and State led to the rebuilding of cathedral and abbey churches in the most magnificent fashion. The Norman style, with its massive columns and heavy rounded arches, had been adopted by some English masons before 1066, and is now sometimes called English Romanesque, because plans, though usually Norman, were executed by Englishmen of great artistic skill and inventiveness. The cruciform design with its long nave and square tower over the crossing, can be seen to best advantage at Durham, where building began in 1093. There the engineering problem of supporting the immense weight of a stone roof was solved for the first time.

In social matters the one remaining English bishop, Wulfstan of Gloucester, showed notable leadership by preaching against the Irish slave trade, on which Bristol flourished, and to support him Anselm issued a canon forbidding Christians to take part in it.

The Kingdom and the Duchy

By the end of the century many noble families were faced with the need to divide the ownership of their possessions in Normandy from those in Britain; both required supervision, but none could be in two places at once. It became the custom to leave Norman estates to the eldest son and those in Britain to the second son.

William the Conqueror, much against his will, decided on his death bed to do likewise. He left the duchy to his eldest son Robert, whose incompetence and disloyalty precluded him from having the kingdom as well; the kingdom therefore went to his second son, William Rufus. To his third son, Henry, he left a large sum of money. The Conqueror's feudal overlord, the King of France, welcomed this settlement, expecting that it would divide the brothers and weaken a family he greatly feared; and so it turned out. In 1088 Rufus had to face a serious rebellion stirred up by Robert, but was able to suppress it. When Robert decided to join the first Crusade in 1096, and as usual needed money, he pledged the duchy to Rufus for three years in return for 10,000 marks of silver. As a Crusader he redeemed his reputation, and when Jerusalem was captured in 1099, he was offered, but refused, the crown of the new kingdom. He was on his way home when in 1100 he heard that Rufus had been killed in the New Forest, and that Henry had seized the royal treasury at Winchester and been crowned at Westminster.

CHAPTER FOUR

The Twelfth Century

The Monarchy

England		Scotland	
Henry I	1100–1135	Edgar	1097–1107
Stephen	1135–1154	Alexander I	1107–1124
*Henry II	1154–1189	David I	1124–1153
*Richard I	1189–1199	Malcolm IV	1153–1165
*John	1199–1216	William the Lion	1165–1214

*Also Lords of Ireland

Anglo-Scottish Relations

For the first part of this period the Border was quiet. Edgar, like his predecessor Duncan II, was clearly a vassal of the English King. Both had been educated in England and won Scotland with English aid. In 1100 Edgar's sister Matilda married Henry I, and Alexander I, Edgar's brother, married Sybilla, one of Henry I's many illegitimate children. David I, a third brother, however, could not resist the opportunity to meddle in English affairs. He had sworn to Henry I to support the claim of the Empress Matilda to be Queen of England (both the Empress and King Stephen's wife Matilda were nieces of David I). On invading England in 1138 David I was decisively defeated in Yorkshire at the Battle of the Standards (the banners of four saints carried by the English army, St Peter of York, St John of Beverley, St Wilfred of Ripon and St Cuthbert of Durham).

In 1149, the prospective heir to the English crown, Henry of Anjou, swore to David that he would allow the Scottish border to include the area of the modern counties of Northumberland, Cumberland and Westmorland, a promise that he conveniently ignored in 1157 when making a treaty with David I's grandson, the boy-king Malcolm IV. William, later called the Lion, Malcolm's brother and successor, was therefore easily persuaded to aid a rebellion against Henry II. He was captured at Alnwick and appeared before the English king with his feet shackled beneath his horse's belly. After a period in prison in Normandy, he obtained his release by recognising Henry as his overlord. This lasted until Henry II's death, and then Richard I, wishing to secure the border during his absence on crusade, freed William from all compacts made with Henry II. In return William later contributed to Richard's ransom.

The Overseas Possessions of the Kings of England

It was the policy of Henry I, as it had been of William Rufus, to dispossess Robert of the duchy of Normandy, and equally Robert's policy to deprive his brother Henry of the kingdom. Henry I, having suppressed a baronial revolt in England fomented by his brother at the beginning of his reign, invaded Normandy in 1106, defeated and captured Robert at Tenchebrai, and held him in honourable confinement in Cardiff Castle for the remaining twenty-nine years of his life. The duchy remained in the possession of the Kings of England for the rest of the century and they did homage for it to their feudal overlords, the Kings of France.

Henry I intended that on his death both the duchy and the kingdom should descend to his daughter Matilda, his son William having been drowned in the Channel Islands. At an early age Matilda had been married to the German Emperor Henry V, but they had no children, and, when the emperor died, she married Geoffrey, Count of Anjou, who conquered Normandy in 1144 and made his son by her, the future Henry II, duke at the age of seventeen.

On Henry I's death the English throne was seized by Stephen, Count of Blois, a grandson of William the Conqueror by his daughter Adela, and a civil war resulted between him and his cousin, the Empress Matilda. She had some temporary success, and though she only ruled England for a short time in the middle of the hostilities she was able to get the young Duke of Normandy accepted by Stephen as his successor.

When Henry II became king, he was already master of the duchy of Aquitaine through his marriage to Eleanor, Duchess of Aquitaine, the divorced wife of the King of France, Louis VII. By war and diplomacy he eventually extended his empire till it included Brittany and Ireland in the west, the overlordship of Scotland, and in the south the county of Toulouse. The King of France, who naturally feared a vassal whose French dominions stretched from the Channel to the Pyrenees, said of him: 'Now in Ireland, now in England, now in Normandy, he must fly, rather than go by horse or ship'.

Henry II, called the first of the Plantagenet kings, because his family badge was *planta genista*, a sprig of broom, lived very simply and accepted many hardships in order to supervise the administration of justice throughout his dominions. This was the chief duty of a medieval king, and he performed it with genius.

Towards the end of his reign Henry was plagued by family disputes and jealousies. He had preferred a mistress, the fair Rosamund, to his wife. Eleanor stirred up her three sons to rebel against him. He was in France in 1189 and in dispute with his youngest and favourite son, John, when he caught fever and died.

For Henry II's sons Richard I and John the family's French dominions were also a major concern. Richard, to help in his wars with the King of France, built an almost impregnable fortress on a bend in the river Seine. This was Chateau Gaillard and became his favourite residence. In 1199, when it seemed that he had brought the wars between Normandy and the King of France to an end, Richard was fatally wounded in a minor baronial conflict. He had only been in England for a total of six months in a reign of ten years.

In 1169 and 1170 a group of Norman barons in Wales undertook an invasion of Ireland, ostensibly to restore the deposed and exiled King of Leinster, but actually to conquer the country for themselves. Under Richard de Clare, Earl of Pembroke, they quickly mastered the east coast ports and Henry II, fearing that they might set up a separate kingdom, went over to receive the submission of the Irish chiefs himself, ignoring their complicated native system of land tenure and imagining that they would regard themselves as his feudal vassals. When he was gone, however, the Irish soon converted their Norman conquerors to their own ways, and centuries of misunderstanding and bitter strife ensued between England and Ireland. The Irish, except those living near the east coast, remained virtually independent until the wars and massacres of Tudor times.

Christendom and Islam

Jerusalem and the Holy Places had come under Islamic rule in 637, five years after Mahomet's death, but Christian pilgrims were not prevented from visiting the Holy Places until the fierce and intolerant Seljuk Turks captured the city in 1076. By then there was a great crescent of Islamic princedoms stretching from Saragossa south through Spain, along the north coast of Africa, north through Syria to the Black Sea and the Caspian, and east to the shores of the Indian Ocean. The principal cities of these states were adorned by beautiful mosques, gorgeous palaces and learned universities, and in them all Arabic was a unifying force equal to Latin in power and even more useful in transmitting the results of ancient Greek philosophy. In some places, notably at Toledo in Spain and in the kingdom of Sicily, where Norman soldiers of fortune had won a new empire from the descendants of Arab conquerors, there was in the twelfth century a fruitful meeting of minds between Moslem and Christian that contrasted sharply with the barbarous massacre that followed the entry of the Crusaders into Jerusalem.

At Toledo Christian students found Arabic translations of ancient Greek writings, including the works of Aristotle and Euclid. One of them, Adelard of Bath, who studied there about 1126, translated Euclid's *Elements* and works on algebra and astronomy by Al-Khwarizmi before returning to England.

Euclid's geometry had an immense and lasting influence, more copies of it being made in medieval times than of any other ancient work except the Bible. The syllabus in medieval Christian schools was devoted to the 'seven liberal arts'; grammar, logic and rhetoric made up the first stage, or *trivium*, and geometry, arithmetic, astronomy and music the second stage, or *quadrivium*. These subjects were often taught as a dry-as-dust oral routine, but under Arabic influence geometry and arithmetic made great progress. The advantages of Arabic numerals over the clumsy Roman mixture of digits and letters became obvious to Italian traders in their commerce with Islamic countries and also to learned men. To the many in all ranks of society who could not read or write there seemed a kind of wizardry about men who could calculate in numbers of any size, great or small, with the aid of only ten symbols, the figures 0 to 9.

The closing of the pilgrim routes to Jerusalem led to the first, and by far the most successful, of the eight Crusades which occurred between 1095 and 1275. It resulted in the defeat of the Seljuk Turks in Asia Minor and Syria and the setting up of three Christian princedoms at the eastern end of the Mediterranean. The sea power and trade of three Italian city-states that had supported the Crusade, Venice, Pisa and Genoa, began to increase rapidly. To defend the newly won territories western Europe had to send out a stream of reinforcements, and for this purpose two international orders of knighthood were founded, the Order of St John of Jerusalem, or Knights Hospitallers, whose badge was a white cross, and the Order of the Temple, or Knights Templars, whose badge was a red cross. Many magnificent gifts of land were made to support them, and the first of these grants in England was made by King Stephen's queen, two of whose uncles were in succession Kings of Jerusalem, the most important of the new princedoms.

The Greek or Orthodox Church, with its Patriarch in Constantinople, the capital of the eastern remnant of the Roman Empire, was an object of contempt to the French knights who were the main driving force of the Crusades. The first Crusaders had answered the call of Pope Urban II, a Frenchman, and they were not the sort of men to understand that the Greek Church was much more directly linked with New Testament times than the Roman church and that it would not have been in such danger of extinction through the rising power of Islam but for the unnecessary rejection by the Roman Church of all compromise between their two traditions.

In 1144 a fresh Moslem attack put an end to the most isolated of the three new Christian princedoms. This provoked a second crusade led by Louis VII of France and

Seal of Richard Coeur-de-Lion. This provides exact contemporary evidence of the arms and armour of a knight at the end of the 12th century. A shirt and leggings of chain mail cover his whole body and a cylindrical flat-topped helmet with a vizor and a round crest protects his head. The large shield is curved, the twin-bladed sword extremely heavy, and the spurs dagger shaped. Stirrups were essential for fighting on horseback

Conrad III of Germany; it was a total failure. A generation later, in 1187, the whole Crusader army of the Kingdom of Jerusalem was destroyed in battle by the overwhelmingly superior forces of Saladin the Kurd, and Jerusalem was captured. Saladin was a soldier-adventurer of genius, who eventually united all the Moslem states between the Tigris and the Nile. This new emergency inspired the third Crusade, joined by three reigning monarchs of outstanding ability, Richard I of England, Philip Augustus of France and the Holy Roman Emperor, Frederick Barbarossa, but it accomplished little of political importance apart from the capture of the port of Acre, and a treaty with Saladin permitting Christian pilgrims to visit Jerusalem. The aged emperor was drowned leading his army across a river in Asia Minor before they had reached Acre. On his way home Richard I was made a prisoner by the Duke of Austria, who refused to release him until an enormous ransom, 150,000 silver marks, had been sent from England.

Though the religious and political effects of the Crusades were often deplorable, the benefits that they brought to European commerce were both numerous and far-reaching. The spirit of adventure that they evoked led on to those ocean explorations that made Europe an exchange and mart for the whole world in the twentieth century.

Popes, Kings and Archbishops

The reforming zeal of the Papacy provoked in the twelfth century a number of serious quarrels between the monarchs of Europe and the Church. One of Henry I's first acts on his accession in 1100 was to recall the saintly Anselm from his self-imposed exile; to ask him to do homage for the 'temporalities' of the see of Canterbury; and to receive the ring and crozier, the symbols of his spiritual authority. Anselm at first refused on the ground that a recent Church council in Rome, which he had attended, laid down that the ring and crozier could be conferred only by the Church. A long contest ensued, but this time conducted with perfect courtesy. Anselm, though over seventy years old, again went into exile. On his return he accepted a compromise, consecrating the bishops appointed in his absence and admitting the king's right in subsequent appointments to present men of his choice, provided that the Church gave them the symbols of office.

A more deadly quarrel arose some sixty years later when Henry II, a great lawgiver, having appointed his friend Thomas à Becket, Archbishop of Canterbury, asked him to cooperate in ending the scandal of 'criminous clerks', that is, of criminals who tried to escape punishment by pleading that they were clergy and should therefore be tried by Church, not secular, courts. The test for this 'benefit of clergy' was ridiculously simple— the ability to quote the first verse of Psalm 51 in Latin. As a Church court could not impose a death penalty, many murderers avoided it by being able to repeat this 'neck verse.' Becket refused to aid the king to set this matter right. At Christmas 1170 Becket deliberately broke what seemed to be a private agreement with the king, and Henry pronounced the fatal words: 'Who will rid me of this low-born priest?' Soon after, four knights, thinking to please the king, murdered the archbishop on the altar steps of his own cathedral. This was followed by his canonisation in 1173 and the rapid rise of a cult centred on his tomb at Canterbury, a popular place of pilgrimage until the Reformation in the sixteenth century.

38

The Corona, or Becket's Crown, Canterbury Cathedral. Thomas à Becket, murdered in 1170, was canonised less than three years later. His tomb was already a place of pilgrimage. A new chapel, finished in 1190, was built to house a shrine containing his bones. The Corona contained another relic of the saint and the stained glass in its windows belongs to the same period

After an interval in which the king visited Ireland, he was reconciled with the Church, did public penance at Canterbury (though he denied responsibility for Becket's death) and promised to support 200 knights engaged in the defence of Jerusalem for one year. He also pledged himself to go on crusade; later, instead of 'taking the Cross,' he endowed three monasteries. Appeals on ecclesiastical matters he agreed should continue to go to Roman courts, where they became a valuable source of income to the Papacy.

In the matter of Church appointments, however, the king's customary powers remained unaffected, and the men preferred continued to be more commonly administrators than saints or scholars. A medieval bishop usually lived an opulent life sharing the warlike pursuits and field sports enjoyed by the nobility.

The Cistercian Monasteries

Amid all the other religious activity of the age the English abbot of a Benedictine abbey at Citeaux in Burgundy, Stephen Harding, laid the foundations of a new order. He reigned there from 1109 to 1133 and in these twenty-four years monks from Citeaux founded a chain of houses right across western Europe. To keep them in close touch with the mother house Harding made rules for regular visitations, an annual chapter and the strict observance in all its austerity of the ancient Rule of St Benedict, who founded the monastery at Monte Cassino about 525. Splendour in dress and buildings, in which many Benedictine abbeys indulged, was to be avoided and a life of work, prayer and contemplation was to be followed in remote and inhospitable country.

This puritanical outlook soon attracted many new recruits in England, where the first community of 'white monks' (they wore robes spun from undyed wool) was set up at Waverley in Surrey in 1129. Other monasteries of the Cistercian order were founded in conditions of the greatest hardship in the dales of Yorkshire, where the monks eventually taught the local population sheep-farming, a hard and lonely calling; the smell of sheep is pungent and clings to shepherds' clothes and body, making them repellent to fellow human beings.

The Cistercian order prospered so rapidly that by 1152 it had 330 houses scattered over England, France, Germany, Italy and Spain; Waverley had five 'daughter' houses in the south and midlands, and Fountains eight spread over Northumberland, Yorkshire and Lincolnshire.

Only forty years later, however, the early ideals of the order had been forgotten and it was possible for Richard I to say to the organiser of the Fourth Crusade: 'You advise me to dismiss my three daughters, pride, avarice and incontinence; I bequeath them to the most deserving; my pride to the Knights Templars; my avarice to the monks of Citeaux; and my incontinence to the prelates'.

Architecture and Illumination

By the middle of the twelfth century almost all the cathedral churches and the churches of the great Benedictine abbeys had been rebuilt in the English Romanesque style; there are beautiful examples of this at Gloucester and Peterborough. Congregations, standing in the long naves of these stately buildings, attended celebrations of the Mass but rarely received communion except at Easter. Wall paintings and sculpture above the entrances and archways conveyed the lessons of the Bible to the illiterate mass of the population.

Towards the end of the century a new architectural style, now called Early English, was adopted. Its tall lancet windows, slender columns and pointed arches combined lightness with strength and inspired masons to create buildings of an airy spaciousness not previously dreamt of.

Two beasts carved early in the 12th century to adorn the Norman cathedral at Salisbury

In the writing rooms of the monasteries the art of manuscript illumination reached new heights. At Winchester a magnificent Bible was made for Bishop Henry of Blois with two full-page drawings measuring 23 by 16 inches and many initial letters adorned with illustrations taken from contemporary life. New books on natural history, a subject in which the works of Aristotle had aroused great interest, were also decorated with miniature paintings. A book of this kind by Alexander Neckham, a foster-brother of Richard I, is remarkable for its freshness and objectivity.

The English language continued to flourish as the mother tongue of the majority, Norman French being restricted to the court and nobility and Latin being used in the services of the Church and in many written records. An English poem entitled *The Owl and the Nightingale* has survived from this time (1195); it puts into the mouths of the two birds a lively satire and quotes fully from the ninth-century proverbs of King Alfred.

41

CHAPTER FIVE

The Thirteenth Century

The Monarchy

England		Scotland	
John	1199–1216	William the Lion	1165–1214
Henry III	1216–1272	Alexander II	1214–1249
Edward I	1272–1307	Alexander III	1249–1286
		Margaret, Maid of Norway	1286–1290
		*John Baliol	1292–1296

*Deposed

Magna Carta and the Papacy

In modern times Magna Carta has become a potent symbol of 'liberty under the law' in every country to which the British legal system has been transplanted, but from the first it was a royal promise to keep the law rather than in itself a statute. From pre-

A section from the Articles of the Barons, the actual document negotiated between King John and the barons in rebellion against him when they met at Runnymede in June 1215. The clause beginning on the fifth line states in Latin:

'No free man shall be arrested or imprisoned or dispossessed or outlawed or exiled or in any

conquest times the kings of England on their accession had been accustomed to issue charters summarising the laws and customs which they intended to preserve, and Magna Carta was a document in this tradition. It was issued near the end of John's reign in the midst of a civil war. As soon as its terms were agreed at Runnymede on 15 June 1215 between King John and the barons in rebellion against him, thirteen copies are known to have been made and distributed, and there may have been more. Four of these have survived, besides the actual document, called the Articles of the Barons, used in the negotiations. King John died in 1216, and by 1225 Magna Carta had been reissued, with modifications, five times, a sign that it was regarded as highly important. In modern times it has been divided into numbered clauses, and in the 39th of these the king, using the royal 'we', promises not to proceed against any free man among his subjects 'save through the lawful judgement of his peers and the law of the land'; and in the 40th he states: 'To no one will we sell, to no one deny or delay, right or justice.'

In Magna Carta the Latin word *liber* (a free man) did not have the significance of the later phrase 'free-born Englishman'. In the sparse, and mainly agricultural, population of the thirteenth century only about one third were free men; the rest were 'tied to the land' and to their feudal lords by a network of customary duties and rights evolved over centuries to suit local conditions. Nor did the word *pares* (peers) provide the protection that trial by jury affords in modern times.

Yet, however many the qualifications that are entered against the view that Magna Carta significantly advanced the cause of liberty, it did undoubtedly from the beginning set a significant limit to the arbitrary power of the monarch. Modern writers who demonstrate that King John's reputation has suffered unfairly through the malignity of monkish chroniclers and that he was in fact a cultivated man deeply interested in the day-to-day business of the law courts—all of which is correct—cannot deny that he

way proceeded against; we (the royal "we", meaning King John) will not put, or cause to be put hands upon him, except by the legal judgement of his peers or by the law of the land.' The next clause reads:
'To no man will we sell, to no man will we deny or delay right or justice.'

43

was on occasions, like almost all the Plantagenets, transported by insane and cruel rages; that he was, more than most men, full of inconsistencies, and that it is the key requirement of a legal system that it should be consistent.

Fortunately for England the Papacy at the time was held by a young man of outstanding legal and political ability, Innocent III, who was determined to be the judge of kings. At the University of Paris one of the best scholars he had met was an Englishman, Stephen Langton, and now he appointed him Archbishop of Canterbury, rejecting two candidates proposed in England. King John was furious, regarding this as gross interference in an internal matter. The Pope placed the country under an interdict, priests being forbidden to perform the services of the Church. The king remained obdurate until, in 1211, the Pope excommunicated him and the King of France prepared to make 'a holy war' against him. Then John, by a cynical reversal of policy, accepted Stephen Langton as Archbishop and his chief adviser. This was a wise choice, for Langton was mainly responsible for drawing up Magna Carta. At the same time the king, posing as a repentant son of the Church, transferred the kingdom to the papacy, making the Pope his feudal overlord and claiming his protection against all enemies of the realm. Innocent III, when news of Magna Carta reached him, denounced it as infringing the rights of kingship and released all concerned from the oaths sworn at Runnymede. Nothing could have caused John's opponents more dismay; they could no longer claim to be 'the army of the Church'. In the ensuing civil war, in which the country was invaded by a French army, John with the aid of Flemish mercenaries was gaining the upper hand when he died of a sudden fever. Innocent died in the same year and his successor, Honorius III, became guardian of John's nine-year-old son, Henry III. The boy was protected by William, Earl of Salisbury, an aged but very able counsellor who had served Henry II and both his sons, and by Stephen Langton. Together they succeeded in driving the French from the country and re-establishing royal authority on the basis of Magna Carta, which, since circumstances had changed entirely since 1215, was a valuable asset to the monarchy during the king's minority.

The Beginnings of Parliament

Throughout Europe the thirteenth century was a period of intense effort and experimentation in politics, religion and business. In few other periods were so many old institutions adapted for new purposes or so many new corporate bodies created, and Parliament at this time owed much to the genius of a French nobleman of far-reaching intelligence and indomitable spirit—Simon de Montfort, Earl of Leicester. When he fiirst came to England as a young man he fell in love with, and secretly married, Henry III's sister Eleanor, a widow of twenty-three. Two years later he went on crusade with the king's brother, Richard of Cornwall, and greatly distinguished himself. On his return he met the king in France, and finding him engaged on a wasteful expedition to recover territories seized by the French, took the part of a candid friend and rebuked him sternly, something the king, a sensitive and highly artistic man, could not bear. Later quarrels over money estranged the former friends still further, and in 1264 led to civil war. Simon, having raised an army against the king, defeated him at Lewes in

Seal of Simon de Montfort, Earl of Leicester AD 1258. Such impressions were made on beeswax, warmed to make it soft, and are an early example of portraiture, done during the lifetime of the owner of the seal. Simon is shown holding his hunting horn to his lips and accompanied by his dog

Sussex in 1264, and captured the heir to the throne, the future Edward I. He then summoned a 'parliament' of his supporters and included, by an innovation not repeated until 1275, two burgesses and two knights from each of a number of boroughs and shires. Less than a year later Edward, the king's heir, escaped, and defeated Simon's forces at Evesham, Simon being killed in action.

Edward I was probably the most gifted of all the medieval kings of England. His orderly mind and towering ambition carried the development of the king's household into an organ of government further than any previous monarch. Parliament became a regular extension of his court, a place where he could discuss his policies with a much wider circle than his immediate entourage. Here his conquest of Wales and attempted conquest of Scotland, enterprises typical of his empire-building spirit, were presented as necessary to the welfare of the realm and taxes imposed to pay for a succession of campaigns were made to appear fair and reasonable. He summoned parliaments to meet after Easter and Michaelmas in nearly every year between 1274 and 1286. It is not known at how many of these knights and burgesses were present, but they certainly attended in 1275 and 1283. Not all were called to Westminster; when the rebel Welsh prince David was captured and tried at Shrewsbury, a parliament was summoned there and witnessed his brutal execution. Parliament began in fact as 'a high court' and only gradually acquired other important functions such as the power to discuss taxation.

Towards the end of Edward I's reign the development of Parliament was endangered by the most serious of all the medieval contests between king and pope. In 1296 Pope Boniface VIII, in the Bull *Clericis laicos*, forbade clergy on pain of excommunication to contribute to royal exchequers money for lay purposes. In his view it was for the

Church, not kings, to decide what enterprises it would support. In England the Archbishop of Canterbury, Robert Winchelsey, an old and loyal friend of Edward I, was in a dilemma; he could not ignore the Bull, but the king was preparing an expedition to Flanders and in urgent need of money. As on many occasions in the past, Edward had demanded taxes from the whole nation, including the Church, and forbade sentences of excommunication to be delivered. Then news came of a rebellion in Scotland; the archbishop was able to argue that this new emergency justified contributions from the Church; and when Parliament met the lords spiritual and temporal continued to function as one body.

Parliament of Edward I. An MS illustration showing the king with King Alexander III of Scotland and the Archbishop of Canterbury on his right, and Llywelyn, Prince of Wales, and the Archbishop of York on his left. In the assembly the lords in black hats are outnumbered by the bishops and abbots in their mitres. The royal officials in the centre are seated on woolsacks

Edward I and the Affairs of Wales and Scotland

Ever since the reign of William the Conqueror Norman families, granted lands in the marches, or borders, of Wales, had been extending their estates, striking inland from the coast, building castles at the heads of valleys, training the Welsh to work and fight for them, and regarding themselves as monarchs of all they surveyed from the high walls of their ancestral homes. Only in the mountains of Snowdonia and central Wales were Welshmen still living under princes of their own race. To them the weakness of Henry III's government seemed to afford an excellent chance to win their independence. Llywelyn, the last of a long line of Welsh princes, supported Simon de Montfort against the king and asked the hand of Simon's sister Eleanor in marriage. As a proud son Edward did not forget such favour to a rebel against his father's throne; he seized Eleanor on her way to Wales, and when the Welsh in reprisal attacked the lords of the Marches, Edward organised so massive a campaign that Llywelyn sued for peace and agreed to pay him homage. In return Edward released Eleanor and consented to her marriage.

The peace did not last; in 1282 Llywelyn and his brother David rebelled together, and Edward, outraged by such treachery, determined to put an end to Welsh independence. In the ensuing war the spearmen of the Welsh princes were shot to pieces by longbowmen recruited in Wales and trained by the lords of the Marches. It was the first of many campaigns to be won by this new and deadly weapon. Llywelyn was killed in a skirmish and decapitated; his head was displayed at the Tower of London. David, who attempted further resistance, was betrayed by Welshmen, tried, condemned and executed.

An Act of Parliament, the Statute of Wales, passed in 1284, created six new shire governments of the English kind—Caernarvon, Merioneth, Flint, Carmarthen, Cardigan and Anglesey, the island that had been the 'bread bowl' from which the Welsh rebels drew supplies. At Caernarvon Edward built the most splendid of a ring of fortresses encircling Snowdonia, a town planted with English settlers and a huge castle within the town walls. The success of his campaigns here and in Scotland was in part due to his employment of a fleet to maintain his supplies and cut off those of the enemy. Politically, however, his treatment of Wales was ill-judged; in 1287 and again in 1292 there were sudden and deadly rebellions, which could only with difficulty be suppressed.

In 1291 the succession to the crown of Scotland was in dispute between two barons of Anglo-Norman descent, John Baliol and Robert Bruce, and Edward I was asked to examine their claims. One hundred and four commissioners appointed to do so decided in favour of John Balliol, who then did homage to Edward and was crowned king. This confirmed in the most open and solemn manner Edward I's position as the rightful overlord of the Scottish kingdom and in his view subsequent rebellions were intolerable. William Wallace, who defeated the English at the battle of Stirling Bridge in 1297 and made himself master of Scotland, roused Edward to the same anger as Llywelyn had done. He resolved to end Scottish independence and the following year went north with a powerful army, and, attacking Wallace's forces on a battlefield of their own choice, inflicted a crushing defeat. Soon Edward had mastered the whole country south

Conway Castle. This fortress, built by Edward I on the mainland guarded the entrance to the Menai Strait from the north. Opposite on the shore of Anglesey stood another Edwardian Castle, Beaumaris. Round towers were preferred because mining under the corner of a square tower could bring down two walls at once. The metal structure on the right is an experimental tubular railway bridge designed and built by Robert Stephenson

of the Forth, and it seemed only a matter of time before Scotland like Wales became an English province. To symbolise this change Edward took south to Westminster the Stone of Scone on which the kings of Scotland had hitherto been enthroned.

Neither in Wales nor in Scotland did race or language divide Edward's friends from his foes. The leaders of rebellion there were no less eager to extend their power than the king himself, and they exacted from their own people feudal obedience no less strict than that which he demanded of them. Unfortunately the king's mind was set in the past; he seems to have regarded himself as King Arthur re-incarnated, a Christian king surrounded by his knights, dispensing justice and defending his subjects from all rebels and traitors. He actually went to Glastonbury with his queen to witness the solemn re-burial of what were alleged to be the bones of Arthur and Guinevere. Such a man could not recognise in himself a great innovator, which he was, both in war and in every branch of government; nor could he understand his opponents' unreasoning and unreasonable attachment to the soil of their native land and their desire to enjoy it unmolested no matter what the cost. The slow and complicated rhythms of life, evolved in Wales and Scotland out of the hard struggle against inclement weather and infertile

48

soil after centuries of raid and counter-raid by sea and land, could not be adjusted to foreign laws or the ways of foreign governors, and attempts at enforcement only united men of different rank and varied interests in opposition to the might of the English.

The Coming of the Friars

Four new religious brotherhoods—their members were called friars—established themselves in Britain during the thirteenth century. Unlike the monks, the friars, as both their friends and their enemies declared, took the world for their cloister; worked in towns rather than the country; owed no allegiance to bishop or parish, though often welcomed by them; were not attached to any one 'house'; and at first refused permanent endowments in the form of property.

Of the four orders the Franciscans, or Grey Friars, were the most influential, adhering closely to the teaching of their founder, the Italian saint, Francis of Assisi (1181-1226); and the Dominicans, or Black Friars, founded by Dominic (1170-1221), a Spanish saint, the best organised. The third order, the Carmelites, was founded in honour of the Blessed Virgin Mary of Mount Carmel; and the Austin Friars, or Order of Friars Hermits of St Augustine, formed a union of various small congregations of hermits. A party of Dominicans, probably from France, settled at Oxford in 1221 (their order was established at Bologna and Paris, both famous for their universities). Three years later a band of Italian Franciscans founded settlements at Canterbury, London and Oxford, and by the end of the century there were over fifty Franciscan centres in England and at least four in Scotland.

The Dominicans and Franciscans soon became as renowned for learning as for holiness; those at Oxford had as their first lecturer Robert Grosseteste (1175-1253), a most distinguished scholar, who became Bishop of Lincoln in 1235, and later an intimate friend of Simon de Montfort. His most famous pupil was Roger Bacon, whose wide-ranging intelligence and speculative mind brought him into conflict with orthodox teachers. His work on optics and the refraction of light through lenses led to the development of spectacles, and among many other projects he discussed the possibility of automobiles, aeroplanes and submarines.

Oxford in Bacon's time was still without college buildings; students began university life at 12 or 13 and lived in the town, which they often terrorised with their bows and arrows. Lecturers had to be popular as well as learned to attract their attention. Walter de Merton, Edward I's chancellor and founder of Merton College, Oxford, demonstrated a better way, creating the first self-governing corporate body of students and teachers with a warden to rule them and the legal right to own property.

Westminster Abbey and Salisbury Cathedral

The abbey church at Westminster, the place which above all others contains the essence of English history, was begun by Henry III when he was thirty-eight, and on the day of Saint Edward the Confessor, 13 October 1269, when the choir and transepts were dedicated, the Confessor's coffin, borne by Henry, his brother and his sons, was carried to its new resting place. In his devotion to St Edward the king had persuaded the monks

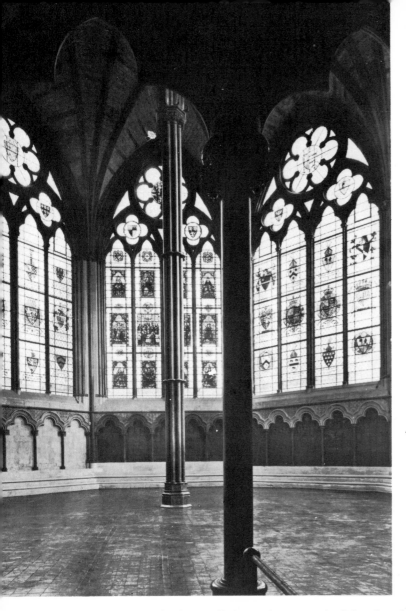

The Chapter House, Westminster Abbey, finished for Henry III's Great Council in 1257. The architect was Henry de Reyns, who also designed the choir and transepts of the Abbey church and intended this room for state assemblies as well as the conduct of abbey business. After 1352 it was frequently used for meetings of the House of Commons. The stained glass in the windows, destroyed by German bombs in 1941, has been restored by Miss Joan Howson

to let him pull down the east end of the church completed by the Confessor in 1065 and replace it by the present building. For architect the king chose Henry of Reyns, who may have been a Frenchman. When he died in 1253, he was succeeded by John of Gloucester and Robert of Beverley.

The new shrine of the Confessor, the work of Italian craftsmen, was adorned with the figures of kings and angels wearing diadems of precious stones, many of them the personal gift of the king. The light of the candles burning above it was reflected in a shining pavement of Cosmati work. Today only the bare shell of the shrine remains; the rest was stripped at the Reformation on the orders of Henry VIII's commissioners.

At the crossing of the transepts, which were also completed by Henry III, was the place of coronation, the same spot where William the Conqueror had received the crown of St Edward. To the east the vaulting of the choir hangs like a canopy in stone a hundred feet above the altar and the shrine. The nave, though in the same style, was not completed until almost the end of the Middle Ages. That a building of such height and weight could stand on a swampy island at the side of the Thames is proof of the skill that went into the Confessor's own church, for the later builders used its foundations.

At Salisbury the cathedral, also built in the new style, was completed with extraordinary speed, the foundation stone being laid in 1220 and Henry III attending the consecration in 1260. The main fabric with its pointed arches and slender pillars shafted with dark Purbeck marble is one of the masterpieces of Nicholas of Ely. The adjoining cloisters, designed by Richard Mason and forming one of the most beautiful quadrangles in the country, were begun in 1264. The spire, 404 feet tall, was not added until the fourteenth century.

Salisbury Cathedral. A view from the Wiltshire Avon. The spire is the tallest in England

CHAPTER SIX

The Fourteenth Century

The Monarchy

England		Scotland	
Edward I	1272–1307	Robert I (Bruce)	1306–1329
*Edward II	1307–1327	David II	1329–1371
Edward III	1327–1377	Robert II (Stewart)	1371–1390
*Richard II	1377–1399	Robert III	1390–1406
Henry IV	1399–1413		

*Deposed

The Affairs of Scotland

The rivalries that had already caused centuries of warfare and misery on both sides of the Scottish border continued into the fourteenth century and grew worse. In 1304 Edward I held a Scottish parliament at St Andrews and there most of the nobility and men of note acknowledged him as king. Stirling Castle, which had been captured by the rebels in 1299, surrendered. William Wallace, who had never acknowledged Edward, was captured, tried at Westminster, and executed. The following year Edward issued an ordinance for the government of Scotland under which Scots and Englishmen were to share authority. But many Scots did not regard Edward as their rightful king and the dispute over the Scottish crown continued. Robert Bruce killed his chief rival, John Comyn, in the Franciscan church at Dumfries, and at once had himself crowned at Scone by the Countess of Buchan in the presence of the Bishops of St Andrews and Glasgow, but for the next year things went badly for him. He was excommunicated by the Pope for sacrilege at Dumfries; one of his brothers, Nigel, and his chief supporter, the Earl of Atholl, were caught and hanged by the English; and the bishops were imprisoned. After some months in hiding he went into action again in 1306, harassing Edward's forces and provoking him to assemble one more great army. Edward, prostrated by a long illness, and lying near Carlisle at the point of death, ordered his son and successor, Edward II, to carry his bones into Scotland at the head of his men. Bruce is reputed to have said he feared his old enemy dead more than he feared the new king living.

Edward II, however, was soon involved in troubles in England, and could not attend to Scottish affairs until 1314. Then he led a large army into Scotland and met Bruce's forces near Stirling; the English, caught in marshes at the mouth of the Bannock Burn and unable to deploy their longbowmen, were decisively defeated, Edward escaped with some of his household, but many English nobles were killed or captured. With ransom money and loot from the English camp the Scots boasted that they had become 'rich in a day'.

Bruce, now in fact, as well as name, King Robert I, was still under ban of excommunication, and in 1320 the Pope summoned four Scottish bishops to Rome to account for their support of him. To this Bruce's chancellor, the Abbot of Arbroath, drafted an eloquent reply in Latin and over forty Scottish nobles sent him their seals, which were

The Ruins of Arbroath Abbey, Angus. Like many abbeys throughout Britain it was 'dissolved' during the Reformation. Arbroath is on the sea coast east of Dundee and the monks used to put a lamp in the circular window of their church as a guide to sailors. The lower part of the window frame can be seen in the centre of the picture

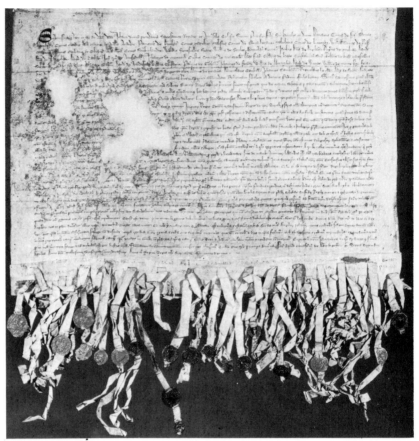

The Declaration of Arbroath, sometimes called Scotland's 'Declaration of Independence'. Drawn up by the Abbot of Arbroath, it declares the Scots' intention to be free even if King Robert should attempt to conciliate the English. The seals indicate the number of 'signatures' obtained

duly affixed to the letter. This, dated 6 April 1320, is now regarded as Scotland's declaration of independence, because the abbot referred to 'our own nation' which 'journeyed from Greater Scythia', and, while professing loyalty to King Robert, insisted that if he allowed the English to subvert his kingdom, the signatories would still 'never, on any conditions, be subjected to the lordship of the English, for we fight not for glory, nor riches, nor honours, but for freedom alone, which no good man gives up except with his life'. The deposition of Edward II by his wife and her lover was worth much more to King Robert than these words; he at once raided Northumberland and began making grants of land there to his supporters; the English queen made peace, acknowledging the independence of the kingdom of Scotland. The peace was of course to be 'final and perpetual'. In 1328 the Pope wrote to 'our dearest son Robert, illustrious King of Scotland' raising the ban of excommunication. By the time this reached Scotland Bruce was dead, and his five-year-old son David had been made king, though he was not crowned till 1332.

The regents appointed to rule in the boy David's name were incompetent; the Scots whom his father had disinherited for disloyalty returned, and Edward Balliol was even crowned at Scone before the Scots rallied to expel him. He went to England and persuaded Edward III to bring an army to Scotland to restore him. At Berwick-on-Tweed the Scots were overwhelmed by longbowmen and David was hurried away to France for safety. Until the English became involved in war with France it seemed likely that they would retain their grip on Scotland. During the Crécy campaign in 1346 David, now twenty-two, returned to Edinburgh, raised an army and ravaged south of the border as far as Durham. There he met a well-organised English army and, after fighting bravely, was captured. He afterwards blamed his defeat on the cowardly conduct of Robert, High Steward of Scotland, who had fled from the battle and been made regent, ruling Scotland for eleven years while negotiations dragged on for the release of David, who seems to have been willing as the price of freedom to acknowledge Edward as his overlord. The Scots, however, preferred to keep their independence and to promise a large ransom to be paid in instalments. In 1371 when David died, childless, only a fraction of this had been paid and the rest was withheld.

Robert II, the first Stuart, David's successor, a man of fifty-five with little capacity for kingship, owed his crown to a lucky marriage, and suffered much insolence from nobles who considered themselves of better birth than he. The border was, as ever, constantly fought over; in a short campaign in 1385 Richard II led an army to Edinburgh and back, burning the abbeys of Melrose and Newbattle on the pretext that they supported the wrong side in the Papal Schism. While the English ravaged the Lowlands, an army of French mercenaries, sent to aid the Scots, a service they hated, raided Cumberland in search of loot. It seemed that this internecine bloodshed would never cease.

The Hundred Years' War

Intermittent hostilities between England and France continued from the reign of Edward III to that of Henry VI (1422-1461) and bred an ill-will between the two countries that lasted long after the end of the Middle Ages. Yet trade between Britain and the Continent, already vigorous when the war began, was little affected by hostilities. Every year the wine fleet sailed under convoy from Bordeaux. Salt from the island of Oléron was an essential import, and vast quantities of English wool entered Flanders via Calais to supply the looms of Bruges, Ghent, Arras, Amiens and other thriving towns.

At the time of the outbreak of war, however, there is no doubt that both sides believed that conquest would benefit trade. In 1336 the Count of Flanders, acting on orders from Philip VI, King of France since 1328, arrested all Englishmen travelling or working there. Edward III at once stopped the export of English wool, provoking a successful revolt against the count in Ghent, a self-governing Flemish cloth town, led by a brewer, Jacob van Artevelde, who appealed to Edward for help. The king then issued his claim to be the rightful king of France, since his mother had been the daughter of Philip IV. He can scarcely have believed in his own claim, but it made a high-sounding reason for levying war taxes in England. War was now a most expensive undertaking; his grandfather Edward I, the first medieval king to pay all his troops on war service, had taught the importance of the longbow, and Edward III perfected it. Early in the campaign he won a sea battle at Sluys that gave him command of the Channel.

The height of English power in France in the fourteenth century was reached between the victories at Crécy in 1346 and Poitiers in 1356. After Crécy Calais was captured and remained an English town until 1558, and after Poitiers King John of France was taken prisoner with about 2,000 other Frenchmen, and remained in captivity until his death eight years later, his kingdom being so ill-organised that it could not raise the huge ransom demanded.

The English were now seen abroad as the first military power in Europe; even their enemies noted that they regarded themselves as invincible; later defeats were attributed to treachery or witchcraft. Their war gains, however, faded away; in 1360 the king made a treaty with the French at Bretigny, where, in return for giving up his claim to the French crown, he was recognised as sovereign Duke of Aquitaine. His son, the Black Prince, set up his court in Bordeaux as his viceroy, but the French constantly plotted a further advance.

Medieval French vineyard. In the centre a picker carries a hod of harvested grapes to the press, where a man stands ready to crush out the juice with his feet. On the left wine-tasters sample the vintage and a merchant bargains over the price. In the foreground men prune the stripped vines

56

The Castle of Ghent, birthplace of John of Gaunt (Ghent), third son of Edward III. Ghent stood near the confluence of the Lys and the Scheldt and was one of the most prosperous of the Flemish cloth manufacturing towns until silt closed its waterway to seagoing ships. The weavers relied on English wool

When war was renewed in 1369, the Black Prince's brother John, Duke of Lancaster, led an unsuccessful expedition to France, and by 1375 the Breton general Bertrand du Guesclin had, by moving his forces swiftly from place to place, achieved by surprise more than any one battle could have given him—only Bayonne, Bordeaux and Calais remained in English hands. Edward, who had been both admired and loved by the whole nation, was prematurely senile, and his son, once a great general, burdened with the sickness which killed him before he could inherit the throne.

The Peasants' Revolt, 1381

> *When Adam delved and Eve span*
> *Who was then the gentleman?*

This was the text chosen by John Ball, a renegade priest, in June 1381 when he preached on Blackheath to the Kentish rebels who had broken into the Archbishop's prison in Canterbury two days before, and released him. He knew that this couplet went to the core of their grievances—his audience were determined to assert their freedom, to be quit of the feudal customs that forced them to work on particular manors for particular lords. Some landowners were already paying gangs of itinerant labourers who demanded rates well above the local average for seasonal work, but whether tied or free the peasants who that summer suddenly converged on London from Kent and Essex were far from destitute of goods or brains; they were poor, of course, but they came from rich and fertile counties, bearing woodmen's axes, hedgers' bills and reapers' hooks, and had chosen at Maidstone a forceful leader to command them, Wat Tyler, who may have been an ex-soldier, and certainly exercised a crude but effective discipline.

The advisers of the boy king Richard II were taken by surprise. The immediate cause of the revolt was the injustice of a new flat rate poll tax; the collectors were harrying the needy, while the rich got off lightly. The rebels, however, were genuine revolutionaries, eager to provide an alternative government, declaring that if Richard had not been misled by his uncle, John of Gaunt, and the rest of his council, he would not need new taxes, and the country would not be in danger of a French invasion (the rebels refused to allow those living within a day's march of the coast to join them, preferring that they should stay and guard the homeland). They also knew their Bibles well enough to see that the wealth and ostentation of the higher clergy were incompatible with the Gospel.

While the Kentish men threatened the capital from south of the Thames, the men of Essex came in to Mile End and camped there within sight of the city walls. London Bridge was not defended, and for nine days the city and the fine houses on its outskirts were at the mercy of the rebels. One band under Jack Straw went to Highbury and set fire to the lord treasurer's house; others looted the palace of the Savoy, John of Gaunt's London home, and then blew it up with gunpowder. The headquarters of the Knights of St John at Clerkenwell burnt for seven days. Foreigners and lawyers caught on the streets were promptly assassinated.

Richard II, who had taken refuge in the Tower, and seen the fires raging in all directions, heard that the rebels wished to see him and courageously rode out to Mile End with the Lord Mayor, William Walworth, and a few companions. At his approach the rebels knelt, saying: 'Welcome, King Richard, we wish no other king but you.' A petition was then handed to him, asking that villeinage should be ended, land made available at a rent of 4d an acre, and traitors executed—demands to which the king gave his consent. Meanwhile the Tower of London was betrayed to the rebels, who dragged out the Archbishop of Canterbury and the lord treasurer and murdered them on Tower Hill. The king met the rebels again, this time at Smithfield. William Walworth, seeing Wat Tyler, who was drunk, insulting the king, slew him on the spot; and the king, seizing the moment, rode forward and addressed the rebels. They, confused and dismayed at the loss of their leader, consented to go home and wait till they received justice.

Little justice was done; the authorities, realising how great the danger had been, and learning how there had been riots in many other places, at Norwich, Bury St Edmunds, and St Albans to mention a few, began a series of trials at which about 400 were condemned to death and hanged, including John Ball, who refused to plead for mercy. The leader of the St Albans men, William Grindcobbe, said before execution: 'Hold firm while you can, and have no thought of me or what I may suffer. If I die for the cause of liberty, I shall think myself happy.' The survivors did hold firm; the government had been given a severe shock; after this many landowners preferred to pay labourers on contract rather than insist on the old forced labour; within a century villeinage had faded out of existence; and there were no more peasants in England. This change, which France did not achieve until, in 1789, society was rent by the earthquake of revolution, and Russia did not experience until the first (not the Bolshevik) Revolution of 1917, occurred in England four to five centuries earlier.

It is sometimes said that this great change in English agriculture was accelerated by a shortage of labour following the great pestilence of 1349, sometimes called the Black Death, by which the continent of Europe was also afflicted. The population of England was then about 4,000,000, and of this, many distinguished authors have said, from a third to a half perished. There is no good evidence for such a high mortality, and if any such disaster had occurred, the consequence would have been not a revolt, nor even a revolution, but the total collapse of economic life. There was undoubtedly an outbreak of bubonic plague in that year and possibly one of louse-borne typhus at the same time (the two diseases were not distinguished till the nineteenth century), but the total number of dead can scarcely have exceeded one twentieth of the population.

By What Means to Remove a King?

Edward II, the fourth son of Edward I, succeeded his father at the age of 23, his elder brothers having died young. He was physically strong and handsome, devoted to sport and to the arts but in character quite unsuited for kingship. In 1308 he married Isabella, the twelve-year-old daughter of Philip IV of France, by whom he had two sons and two daughters. Apart from the defeat at Bannockburn, he offended his nobles by the favour he showed to Piers Gaveston, and later the Despenser family, and by his cruelty towards those who rebelled against him.

Towards the end of his reign Queen Isabella, said to have been the most beautiful woman in Europe, became the mistress of Roger Mortimer, one of the Lords of the Welsh Marches, and with him she forced Edward to abdicate in favour of his son, who was crowned Edward III at the age of fifteen. Edward II was imprisoned in Berkeley Castle in Gloucestershire and soon afterwards died in mysterious circumstances.

Seventy years later Henry Bolingbroke, Duke of Lancaster, returned from exile, made his cousin Richard II his prisoner, arranged that he should abdicate publicly and transfer power to him as the new and rightful king. Soon afterwards Richard II died in mysterious circumstances in Pontefract Castle. Edward II's deposition and Richard II's are thus strikingly similar. Their predecessors on the throne had been strong rulers and victorious commanders and their subjects had admired their passion for war, their gorgeous tournaments and costly banquets, and the extravagant ostentation of court apparel.

The friends and companions in arms of Edward I and Edward III could not easily tolerate defeat for as 'peers of the realm' they had almost come to look upon themselves as the peers of the king himself. Certainly they despised and hated men of lesser rank such as Piers Gaveston, and the favourites of Richard II. For these kings to have earned the contempt of their leading subjects was not, however, considered sufficient cause for deposing them. Might must not be seen to be right, and so the depositions were given an air of legality by calling an assembly that closely resembled a parliament and obtaining its consent. This was no more than semi-legal because a true parliament could not be called except by the king, but when Edward II was deposed his undoubted heir was at once crowned, appearances being more easily kept up than in the case of Richard II, whose rival, Bolingbroke, who meant to be king whether by law or usurpation, could not, though of royal blood, lay a reasonable claim to the crown by descent.

The truth is that a country burdened with a bad king can either endure, or suffer a revolution. Both Edward II and Richard II had broken the solemn oaths sworn in the presence of their subjects at their coronations. By 1399 Richard, tainted by megalomania, had behaved with such tyrannical disregard for justice and honour that he had no friends left, and kingship depends ultimately on the character of the monarch. When that shows irremediable flaws, the monarchy itself is in danger, for once kings are seen to be removable, usurpation can become a habit.

The Development of English Architecture

Nothing in the progress of the masons' craft was without justification from the point of view of engineering, and the architects of the later Middle Ages have been ill-served by the Victorian admirers of the Gothic style who applied the term Decorated to the work of the first part of the fourteenth century and Perpendicular to that of the latter part, for the word 'decorated' implies that the builders added useless ornament, and 'perpendicular' that they preferred straight lines to curves. In fact, light, and still more light, was their objective.

English Romanesque designers had brought light through the upper part of their structures, giving churches a full triforium and clerestory. Now, by transferring more of the outward thrust of arches and roofs from walls to exterior buttresses, that were in effect scaffolding in stone, they could afford much wider and grander window openings. In this way the new style gave the glazier and painter of stained glass much larger scope for the exercise of their art, and masons, working on the mouldings round these windows and the fantastically complicated tracery at the heads of window arches, adorned them with naturalistic carvings imitated from the leaves of oak, maple, ivy and vine. All this work was, however, incidental to the engineering necessity of making a window frame durable enough to hold the glass in position against hail and snow, wind and rain. So strong were these medieval buildings that in some parts of the country they even survived the shock of minor earthquakes like the one that in 1382 shook down the Romanesque bell tower of Canterbury Cathedral. The builders worked to honour an eternal God, and built not for their own time, but for eternity.

The stone ceiling bosses, which locked the ribs of the vaulting together, were also richly carved and painted to give the eye a resting place amid the maze of lines, but the boss was also needed as a weight exerting a downward thrust. Towards the end of the

The royal banqueting hall in the palace of Westminster, now used only on ceremonial occasions. Here the body of Sir Winston Churchill lay in state. It formerly housed the royal courts of justice and was the scene of several State trials

century, when the masons at Gloucester Cathedral were making the first experiments in what is now called the Perpendicular style, these bosses were developed into pendants, pulling the ceiling towards them and away from the side walls.

The leading architect of the time, Henry Yevele, was not employed only on ecclesiastical work. Together with a master of timber architecture, Hugh Herland, he re-roofed the royal banqueting hall at Westminster, using the original walls of the hall built for William Rufus, and providing a clear floor space measuring 240 by 68 feet, by heightening and buttressing the walls to bear a new hammer-beam ceiling. For this, huge oak timbers were cut in Alice Holt Forest in Surrey and floated down the Wey and the Thames. When, in George V's reign, this roof was in danger of destruction by deathwatch beetle, a replica was made in oak from the same forest. A white hart, a favourite subject of medieval legend, occurs frequently among the many carvings which adorn the hall. This is the badge of Richard II, the king who had commissioned the building and whose tyrannical behaviour resulted in his being brought there in 1399 as Bolingbroke's prisoner to perform the humiliating act of abdication.

Learning and Literature

In the last half of the fourteenth century learning and literature were much indebted to three very different Englishmen: William of Wykeham, Bishop of Winchester; John Wyclif, an Oxford don; and the poet Geoffrey Chaucer.

Wykeham (1324-1404) was dissatisfied with established ways of education, dominated as they were by the Church, because they were not giving the training needed for work in the royal household, so he built at Winchester a new school, opened in 1382, with buildings of its own for teachers and pupils to live in, and made it a legally independent property-owning corporation.

For those proceeding to university from Winchester Wykeham also built New College, Oxford, which, with bell-tower, cloisters and quadrangle, housed seventy scholars. It was by far the largest Oxford foundation of the century; Exeter College (1314) had thirteen, Oriel (1326) only ten, and Queen's (1341), founded by the chaplain of Queen Philippa, wife of Edward III, twelve. At Cambridge, where peasants burnt the records during the 1381 revolt, there seem to have been fewer students, but seven new colleges were founded during the century, two of which were later absorbed by Trinity, while Clare (1326), Pembroke (1347), Gonville Hall (1349), Trinity Hall (1350), and Corpus Christi (1352) still flourish. Residential foundations were too small to affect the life of the university at first; Oxford had over 1,000 unattached students; but gradually the colleges, being corporate bodies, accumulated such rich endowments from private patrons of learning that they became more important than the university. They put their own stamp on its character, and after nearly six centuries Wykeham's colleges still educate men who become Ministers of State.

New College, Oxford. Planned by William of Wykeham to receive students coming up from his college at Winchester, it was the first residential building of its kind

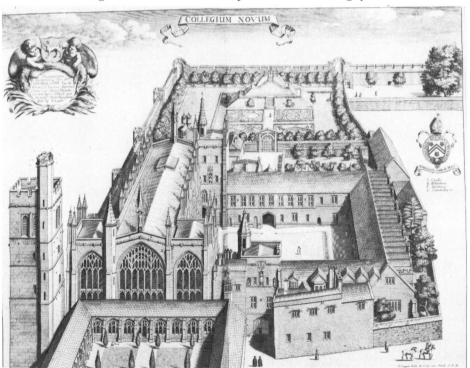

The first chapter of the Acts of the Apostles from the translation of the Vulgate, or Latin, Bible made by Wyclif's followers about 1380-1384, which was the first complete Bible in English

Wykeham was by no means the only devout Christian to realise that the Church needed reform. John Wyclif (1320-1384), from his study of the Bible and its origins, saw that there was no authority in the New Testament for many of the practices of the Church. In addition, to the dismay of all Christians, a schism broke out in the papacy. From 1378 to 1414 there were two popes, each claiming to be canonically elected, one reigning at Avignon and the other in Rome, and each demanding from their adherents as much revenue as previous popes had asked from the whole of Christendom. France, Scotland and Spain supported Avignon; England, Germany and Italy, Rome. Wyclif won much political popularity by publishing pamphlets inveighing against the wealth of the Church and of the popes and urging that Church reform should be ordered by the king not the papacy—a foreshadowing of the Reformation of the sixteenth century. A number of Wyclif's followers, called Lollards, were tried and executed for heresy, and, though criticism of the Church continued to be widespread, no large reforms were attempted.

Geoffrey Chaucer (1340-1400) was not only a poet of the first rank but one of the most learned men of his time, astronomy being one of his many interests. As a young man he fought in the French wars, and what he saw horrified him. After serving the king on diplomatic missions in Italy and Flanders he became controller of customs in the port of London and a member of Parliament. His poetry, which enriched the English language beyond measure, showing the way towards Spenser and Shakespeare, is memorable for the humour and compassion with which he records the virtues and vices of his fellow men and the beauties of the English countryside: Spenser called him 'the well of English undefiled'.

These lines are from the first book printed in England and run as follows:
'*Here endeth the book named the dictes or sayengis of the philosophres enprynted by me William Caxton at Westmestre (Westminster) the yere of our lord MCCCCVII. Whiche book is late translated out of Frenshe into englyssh by the Noble and puissant lord Lord Antone Erle of Ryuyers lord of Scales and of the Isle of Wight, Defendour and directour of the siege apostolique for our holy Fader the Pope in this Royame of Englond and Gouernour of my lord Prynce of Wales And It is so that at suche tyme as he had accomplysshid this sayd Werke it liked him to send it to me in certayn quayers to oversee. Whiche forthwith I sawe and fonde therin many grete, notable, and wise sayengis of the philosophres According unto the bookes made in frenshe Whiche I had ofte afore redd But certaynly I had seen none in englissh.'*
Lord Rivers had been delighted by a copy of the French version shown him by a Gascon knight whom he met during a pilgrimage to the shrine of St James of Compostela in northern Spain

64

CHAPTER SEVEN

The Fifteenth Century

The Monarchy

England		Scotland	
Henry IV	1399–1413	Robert III	1390–1406
Henry V	1413–1422	James I	1406–1437
★Henry VI	1422–1461	James II	1437–1460
Edward IV	1461–1483	James III	1460–1488
Richard III	1483–1485	James IV	1488–1513
Henry VII	1485–1509		

★Deposed

Rebellion in Wales and Scotland

In the fifteenth century internal peace in Britain depended on a delicate balance of power between rival groups of nobles, often closely related by marriage, who ruled their hereditary domains like autonomous princes and were more concerned with maintaining and increasing the area of their estates than with the welfare of the country as a whole. Land, though nowhere intensively cultivated, was the main source of wealth and to acquire vast areas, either by marriage or conquest, offered prizes so much coveted that to win them men and women readily broke the most sacred ties of kinship and hospitality. The sharp wind of 'man's ingratitude' was felt first in this direction then in that as various family groups changed allegiance.

Of the three countries England was immeasurably the richest, and to offset this disadvantage the Welsh and the Scots looked to France, England's ancient enemy and Scotland's ancient ally. Events in France were therefore closely watched, and men knew that any shift of power there would almost certainly lead to changes at the English court. This was first exemplified during the revolt of the Welsh under Owain Glyn Dwr.

In 1400 a quarrel broke out in Wales between Glyn Dwr, a rich and cultured young noble whose lands lay in north Wales, and Reginald Grey, Lord of Ruthin, a member of Henry IV's council. Glyn Dwr ravaged Ruthin, Denbigh, Rhuddlan and Flint before the levies of the counties on the Severn could rally. When they did so, their better arms and discipline were too much for the Welsh, who were defeated. They had, however, gained one valuable prisoner, Edmund Mortimer, a grandson of Edward III and a claimant to the throne of England.

At the time of this revolt Henry IV had just returned from a military expedition to Edinburgh, undertaken to test the loyalty of the Scottish nobles to a king they did not respect, Robert III, who had been a cripple from boyhood. Henry had hoped that he would receive enough support in Scotland to renew the claim of Edward I to English overlord-ship, but none was forthcoming. Two years later the Earl of Douglas, whose lands stretched right across the Lowlands of Scotland, raided Northumberland. He was defeated and taken prisoner at Homildon Hill by one of Henry IV's chief supporters, Henry Hotspur, heir to the Percy earldom of Northumberland, whose bowmen shot the Douglas forces to pieces. Henry IV, though Hotspur had incurred great expense over this campaign, would not let him ransom Douglas and other Scottish prisoners, and this so infuriated Hotspur that the next year with Douglas, Glyn Dwr and Mortimer he plotted a rebellion on the Welsh border. He was intercepted by Henry at Shrewsbury before he could join forces with Glyn Dwr and there defeated and killed. Douglas was captured, but released without ransom in the hope he might later defect.

Glyn Dwr's rebellion was, however, by no means over. Charles VI, King of France, sent him ships to aid in the capture of castles near the seashore like Harlech and Aberyst-wyth, which were taken. Much of south Wales also went over to Glyn Dwr, who then felt strong enough to plot with the Earl of Northumberland the division of Henry's kingdom into three parts, the north and centre to go to the Percies, the west to Glyn Dwr and the rest to Mortimer.

In addition to this threat in Wales Henry had to face a fresh plot against him in the north, organised by Richard Scrope, Archbishop of York, who raised an army but, when the royal forces arrived, allowed himself to be tricked into surrender. He and those of the conspirators who were taken with him were tried by a judge appointed by the king and executed. For an archbishop to be tried by a royal court was contrary both to canon law and to custom, and Henry's action was proof to all his enemies that he meant to keep the crown at all costs. The Earl of Northumberland, who had also been a con-spirator, took refuge first in Scotland, then in Wales, and later in France. In his absence Henry confiscated his lands.

In Scotland Robert III, who had been seriously injured in boyhood by a kick from a horse, had proved incapable of kingship, and the Scottish Parliament had agreed in 1402 that his brother, the ambitious Duke of Albany, should be Regent. Four years later Robert, fearing for the future of his heir, his twelve-year-old son James, decided to send him to the French court. On the voyage James was captured by English pirates and handed over to Henry IV, who kept him in honourable confinement. Albany, when Robert's grief over this mishap caused his death, proclaimed his nephew king as James I, but took no steps to obtain his release.

In 1408 Henry prepared to interfere in the affairs of Scotland still further by allying himself with the head of the Macdonald clan, a man of considerable culture who had been to Oxford and now styled himself Donald, Lord of the Isles, and laid claim to most of northern Scotland. With his clansmen Donald marched on Aberdeen, but the townspeople rallied and defeated them at Harlaw, killing Donald's chief supporter, Hector Maclean. Donald, receiving none of Henry's promised help, remained inactive until his death in 1423, and the Regent felt strong enough after Henry's death to ally himself openly with France against England.

The End of the Hundred Years' War

Henry V, who succeeded his father at the age of twenty-six, had already distinguished himself as a commander in Wales fighting against Glyn Dwr. Unlike the wild romantic figure in Shakespeare's *Henry IV*, he was serious, learned and hard-working. War had given him a taste for glory, and to satisfy it he renewed the claim to the kingdom of France first made by Edward III. He also sought to wipe out the memory of his father's usurpation by releasing the young Earl of March from captivity, restoring the Percy lands to Hotspur's son, and burying Richard II with great pomp in Westminster Abbey.

On 11 August 1415 he crossed from Southampton to the mouth of the Seine with 9,000 men and 1,500 ships and laid siege to Harfleur. The French made no attempt to help the town, which surrendered, after an all-night cannonade by the English artillery, on 22 September. Henry had lost over a third of his men from fighting and sickness, but, suspecting the French to be badly led, risked everything by taking 900 men-at-arms and 5,000 archers on a march north to Calais. He was pursued by a large army, numbering possibly 10,000 and intercepted at Agincourt. There, on St Crispin's Day, 25 October 1415, the French, hemmed in by woods, attacked on a narrow front across rain-sodden ground. Henry had placed his bowmen in protected positions on the flanks and their fire caused terrible losses among the French in their heavy armour. Panic turned defeat into disaster. Among the slain were the Constable of France, seven princes, more than 1,500 knights and possibly 4,000 men-at-arms. The Duke of Orleans was among the many high-ranking prisoners. The English losses were very small, about 300 in all, among them the Duke of York and the young Earl of Suffolk, whose father had died at the siege of Harfleur. This was the army, short of food and tired out by long marches, that Shakespeare celebrated in the line 'We few, we happy few, we band of brothers'.

The king returned to England with his chief prisoners and was welcomed in London on 23 November with splendid medieval pageantry. He was now on fire to conquer the whole of France. During the Agincourt campaign he had benefited from the neutrality of John the Fearless, Duke of Burgundy, a member of the French royal family, whose domains included Flanders with its rich cloth-manufacturing towns. These were England's best customers for wool, and when, in 1419. the French lured Duke John to a meeting and there murdered him, his successor welcomed an open alliance with the English.

By 1420 Henry was strong enough to impose on the French the treaty of Troyes. By this it was agreed that he should be recognised as ruler of western France and, on the death of Charles VI, of the whole country; he was also granted the hand of Charles's daughter Catherine in marriage, and by her had a son, Henry VI.

Charles's son, however, did not accept the treaty of Troyes, and, re-inforced by a large contingent of Scottish mercenaries, attacked and killed Henry's brother, the Duke of Clarence, at Baugé in 1421. Henry was in England when he heard of this disaster, and, speaking of it later, said of the Scots: 'They are a cursed nation; wherever I go, I find them in my beard.' The French, though they later made the Scots' leader, the Earl of Buchan, Constable of France, did not find them easy allies. Between battles they had ferocious appetites and were popularly known as *sacs à vin* and *mangeurs de mouton*. To fight against them Henry returned to France, contracted a fatal illness, and died on 31 August 1422. Even on his death bed he was planning a fresh campaign—a crusade to Egypt.

The death of Charles VI two months after that of Henry gave the French the opportunity to repudiate the Treaty of Troyes. Henry's brother, the Duke of Bedford, in alliance with the Burgundians, proclaimed Henry VI, though only a baby, King of France, but, before the duke died in 1435, a whirlwind had swept away all chances of maintaining the claims of the English royal family to the crown of France.

In 1429 a seventeen-year-old peasant girl from Lorraine, hearing voices and seeing visions, made her way to the Dauphin, raised an army which drove the English from Orleans, and took the Dauphin in triumph to his coronation in Rheims. This was Joan of Arc, but even her miraculous success was no cure for the ills that beset the French court. She was captured fighting against a Burgundian force, sold to the English for 10,000 crowns, and tried before a French bishop; exhausted after many months of prison, interrogation and trial, she confessed to the sin of witchcraft, recanted, and was condemned to be burnt alive, a sentence carried out by the English in Rouen. After this the English suffered many defeats and the Burgundians went over to the French side. By 1453 only Calais remained in English hands. By 1456 Joan's mother had, by long and tireless pleading, persuaded the Church to reverse its judgement on her warrior daughter.

The underlying impulse in the Hundred Years' War, as in every war, had been robbery. Typically Henry's first act after winning Harfleur was to assign English soldiers lands in France. No way other than going to war offered so many opportunities for easy riches to those whose chief skill was in arms and whose capital consisted in a hardy constitution, a horse, a suit of armour, and a two-edged sword. Castles, when faced by armies of robbers, had proved a wholly insufficient defence for those who wished to farm in peace within sight of their walls. These fortresses, so much admired and trusted by military men for four hundred years, were a costly failure, far too expensive for builders to keep in repair, or for their masters to garrison and victual. Few fortresses fell to beseigers; most were betrayed. The heavy suits of plate armour fashionable in the fifteenth century had rendered their owners almost immobile in battle and an easy prey to missiles of all kinds. By 1450 gunpowder menaced both castles and men-at-arms alike, and kings in their wars with feudal princes had tapped a new and immaterial source of strength, something that gave their men a morale that not even bad generals could dissipate—nationalism. The hatred of the whole French population for the English, roused by their pitiless devastation of the richest provinces, was to have consequences of a deadly and mysteriously lasting kind.

The Reigns of James I and James II

In 1424 James I returned to his kingdom after eighteen years of fairly pleasant captivity in England. He was 30, and brought with him as his bride Joan Beaufort, a descendant of

68

John of Gaunt, Duke of Lancaster. They both behaved with ferocity against those noble families who attempted to thwart Stuart ambitions. The young Duke of Albany and his two sons, together with their grandfather, the Earl of Lennox, were beheaded, and in 1428 fifty Highland chiefs were treacherously arrested and imprisoned.

Three years later there was a Highland revolt and the Earl of Caithness, one of James's commanders, was killed during the fighting, but James I was able to restore order. At this time an Italian, later to become Pope Pius II, visited the Scottish court and left an account of its splendour—Linlithgow was turned from a castle into a mansion to please the king. This contrasted sadly with the Italian's record of the squalor in which most Scots lived, in cottages roofed with turf and having ox-hide curtains instead of doors, a people, he said, whose cold land produced so little wheat that even bread was a luxury.

The Douglases, a family always dangerous to the throne, suffered a series of misfortunes at this time. The fourth Earl, having survived the battle of Shrewsbury, was killed in action against the English in France in 1424. His successor was imprisoned following a Lowland rebellion, but when James I was murdered at Perth in 1437, the fifth Earl of Douglas was made Regent for the six-year-old James II. The fifth earl had two young sons and when he died two years later, they were enticed into Edinburgh Castle and murdered there by Sir William Crichton, a friend of the king.

James II took control of affairs in 1449 at the age of nineteen and reigned eleven years. He soon imitated the crime of 1440; having invited the eighth Earl of Douglas to dine at Stirling Castle, he stabbed him to death. A subservient Scottish Parliament officially condoned the deed. The ninth earl fled to England and his three brothers were killed in battle attempting to regain their inheritance. James, now enriched by the former possessions of Douglas, March, Fife, Mar, Buchan, Ross and Lennox, did not live long. A Scottish gun, bursting during the siege of Roxburgh, a border castle held by the English, ended his life when his son and successor, James III, was only nine.

More significant perhaps than all these deeds of blood was the growth of Scotland's oldest university, St Andrews. This was founded in 1412 by the Bishop of St Andrews, and his example was followed by the Bishop of Glasgow, who founded a university there in 1451.

The Wars of the Roses
By 1450 Henry VI, a grandson of Henry Bolingbroke, Duke of Lancaster, who usurped the throne from Richard II, had proved his incompetence, and the two branches of the royal house, Lancaster with its red rose badge, and York with its white, began a series of manoeuvres aimed at getting possession of the king's person and manipulating his prerogatives to their own advantage. As in all ages, supreme power was the glittering prize for which no sacrifice of blood or riches seemed unfitting to men of ambition. These wars were no petty family squabbles; the fate of the nation hung in the balance while they continued, for the protagonists did not hesitate to seek foreign help, and the King of France, to prolong hostilities, gave the Lancastrians some aid, but not enough to ensure their victory. To weaken England, he considered no falsehood or double-dealing out of place.

Richard Beauchamp, Earl of Warwick, with the child king, Henry VI, for whose education he was responsible. His badge, a muzzled bear, is at his feet. He died in 1439 and was buried in the Beauchamp Chapel in St Mary's Church, Warwick, the larger of the two chapels which the artist, John Rous, has drawn. The many quarterings shown on his coat of arms are an indication of the great wealth of the Earls of Warwick

The breakdown of Henry VI's government was due in part to his education. His uncles and guardians did little to train him in the art of ruling men; if they had intended him to be a monk, they would have done well. He became wholly absorbed in such projects as the building of Eton College and King's College, Cambridge, without any realisation of what this involved financially. His administration depended on an elaborate system of borrowing, creditors being assigned particular royal revenues and so being paid by instalments. All these debts were recorded with great care, but in such an intricate and inflexible manner that the king's advisers could never tell at any given time whether the government were solvent or not, and the cash required for the day-to-day expenses of the royal household was often not available.

At no period in history has taxation been popular, but some of Henry VI's sheriffs in their capacity as tax collectors earned an unusual degree of resentment, and in 1450 one caused a revolt in Kent which put London itself in danger. Its leader, Jack Cade, brought several thousand rebels to Blackheath and a royal force, sent by the king to stop him, joined them and marched on London, which they were allowed to enter. The rebels murdered the Lord Treasurer and his son-in-law, the Sheriff of Kent, but found the temptation to rob innocent citizens too great to resist. After a fight on London Bridge they were expelled and persuaded by promises of pardon to disperse. Cade fled, only to be captured and killed by the new Sheriff of Kent. His exploits had demonstrated to more highly placed malcontents the weakness of the government.

During a truce in France in 1445 Henry had married Margaret of Anjou, whose father was a brother of Charles VII, and they had a son, Edward, whose birth in 1453 dampened Yorkist hopes of the succession. The following year, however, the king became insane, and the Duke of York was made Protector. This was not a situation which the beautiful and spirited Queen Margaret would tolerate. Nine months later the king recovered and the duke was soon at war with the queen. He marched on London, defeated the royal army at St Albans and had himself named as Henry's successor. He failed, however, to meet the queen's next attempt against him, and was defeated and killed at Wakefield on 30 December 1460. The duke's head, together with those of his heir and the Earl of Salisbury, were exposed on Margaret's orders on the walls of York. The decimation of the older noble families, one of the main results of these wars, had begun.

Edward, the new Duke of York, a handsome boy of eighteen, soon found a powerful ally in the Earl of Warwick, head of the Neville family, who had vast estates scattered over the whole country and, as Captain of Calais, a private army and navy at his command. In 1461 the duke, having had himself proclaimed Edward IV at Westminster,

The Chapel of King's College, Cambridge, from the south-west. Founded by Henry VI in 1442

went north to attack the queen, who was determined to maintain her husband's cause. Edward, however, advancing in a snowstorm at Towton in Yorkshire, not only defeated the Lancastrians but killed or executed many of their leaders. Over a hundred were deprived of their lands by Act of Parliament.

Edward left the suppression of the remaining Lancastrians to the Earl of Warwick. It took him three years, and when at last Henry VI was captured and imprisoned in the Tower Queen Margaret continued to intrigue against the Yorkists from exile in France. In 1464 Edward fell in love with and secretly married Elizabeth Woodville, the widow of a Lancastrian noble, and by this offended the Earl of Warwick, who had planned he should marry a French princess.

In 1470 the earl decided to change sides, something for which Edward was totally unprepared. For a short time he succeeded in getting both Edward IV and Henry VI into his custody, but though a good king-breaker he was not a good king-maker. Having released Henry VI and had himself made Protector he allowed Edward IV and his brother Richard, Duke of Gloucester (the future Richard III), to escape to Flanders, where, with the help of their brother-in-law, the Duke of Burgundy, they raised an army and returned the next year to fight for the throne. The Duke of Clarence, another brother of Edward IV, who had supported the Lancastrians, went over to the Yorkists, and the Earl of Warwick, in trying to prevent the brothers entering London, was defeated and killed in battle at Barnet on 14 April 1471. The same day Queen Margaret landed in Dorset, and tried to join forces with Jasper Tudor, the uncle of the future Henry VII, in Wales. Edward IV intercepted her army at Tewkesbury and completely destroyed it, killing her young son, the Lancastrian Prince of Wales. Henry VI was executed in the Tower on Edward IV's orders.

In 1483, when Edward IV died, his twelve-year-old son Edward V was at Ludlow Castle on the borders of Wales in the care of his grandfather Lord Rivers, a most accomplished man and a great friend of William Caxton, England's first printer. Edward V's younger brother Richard was with his mother, who took sanctuary with him in Westminster Abbey.

The Duke of Gloucester, however, did not intend that they should stand between him and the crown. He took Edward V away from Lord Rivers, who was executed without trial, and put him and his young brother in the Tower of London, using the Archbishop of Canterbury to get Richard out of sanctuary. Both boys were then declared illegitimate, and probably murdered; they were last seen alive in the Tower. The duke was crowned king as Richard III, but he was unable to prevent his enemies gathering round Henry Tudor, a grandson of Henry V, who was in exile in Brittany. In 1485 Henry landed with an army at Milford Haven on the west of Wales and marched into the Midlands. Richard met them at Bosworth near Leicester, but during the battle he lost most of his forces by desertion to Henry's side and after a brief fight was killed. One story says that the coronet he had worn on his helmet was found on a thorn bush and placed on the head of the victor, who became the first of the illustrious Tudor dynasty.

Bosworth has been called the last battle of the Wars of the Roses, but Henry VII had many perils to face before his throne was secure. He sought peace with the Yorkists by marrying Elizabeth, the young daughter of Edward IV, but some of his enemies supported two low-born imposters who pretended to be Edward V, Lambert Simnel, and Perkin Warbeck. Simnel was able to bring an army over from Ireland, and reached the Midlands, but was defeated by Henry at Newark. Warbeck received help from James IV of Scotland, but also failed. Henry, using new methods of taxation with great success, soon made himself by far the richest man in the kingdom, and, having a monopoly of gunpowder, was seen to be too powerful a monarch for any duke or earl to overthrow.

The Exploration of the Atlantic

The long gestation of astronomical knowledge in the Middle Ages produced in the last half of the fifteenth century a number of astonishing achievements in applied science, chief among them the voyages of Christopher Columbus and John Cabot. The Portuguese seaman Bartholomeo Diaz had in 1488 sailed for 4,500 miles out of sight of the African coast before his discovery of the Cape of Good Hope, the good hope being that India could be reached by sea from Europe. His was, however, a feat of seamanship achieved with caravels, ships better designed than before for ocean-sailing, not a deliberate testing of a geographical theory. Columbus relied on the work of Toscanelli, a fifteenth century Italian geographer, and, instead of looking for an eastward passage to India, searched for one in the west. When he reached the Bahamas on his first voyage in 1492 after sailing only 2,600 miles, he thought that he had done so. It was soon discovered that Toscanelli's calculation of the size of the world had been wildly wrong, but in this case the mistakes of science were as valuable as its successes.

The explorations of Columbus had been assisted by the steady warm air currents soon to be called trade winds. What lay beyond Iceland was not made known to the world until John Cabot, a sailor from Venice, settled in Bristol. He also believed in a westward passage to India and, gaining Henry VII's backing for a voyage in northern latitudes, reached the coast of Newfoundland in 1497. Returning after a short stay, he went back again the next year, touching the mainland in what was later called Nova Scotia. Not for twenty years was it known how vast a land mass America is.

Grammar Schools, Printing and the Universities

Shakespeare in the second part of *Henry VI*, written about 1590, makes Jack Cade say to the Lord Treasurer of England: 'Thou hast most traitorously corrupted the youth of the realm in erecting a grammar school; and whereas, before, our forefathers had no other books but the score and the tally, thou hast caused printing to be used, and, contrary to the king, his crown and dignity, thou hast built a paper-mill.' Shakespeare knew that most rebels are conservatives at heart and are really protesting against change and that grammar schools had indeed provided new opportunities for children of the middle classes. Eton College, founded by Henry VI in 1440, like many other grammar schools established at this time, was by its statutes instructed to house, clothe, feed and educate seventy scholars, and also give free instruction to a number of boys living locally whose parents could pay their other expenses. The statutes said that the seventy scholars should be *pauperes et indigentes* (poor and needy) and should be given a good grounding in religion and sound

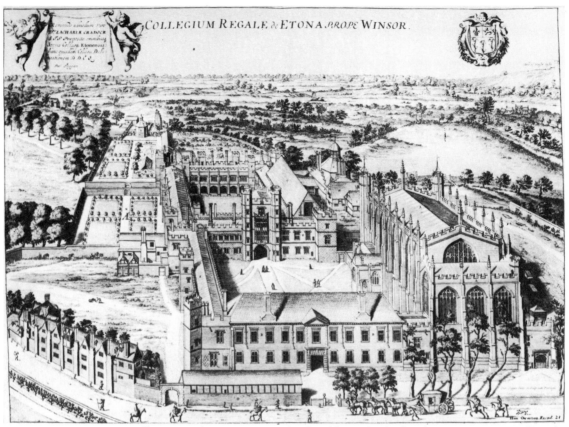

Eton College, an 18th century view. The chapel begun by the founder, Henry VI, is on the right. The brickwork of the gateway in the centre, called Lupton's Tower, and of the cloisters beyond, is some of the earliest to be erected in England

learning. This phrase, however, was intended as a legal protection for the Provost and Fellows, who could not under canon law use funds given for religious purposes except for 'the poor and needy', but this meant in practice the sons of families of some standing. The poor, then and until late in the nineteenth century, looked upon their children as part of their 'labour force' and put them to work as soon as they ceased to be infants; but between the poor and the rich, who usually sent their children away to join the household of some noble family to learn 'manners' and knightly accomplishments, there was a rising middle class, for whom the benefactors who founded pre-Reformation grammar schools intended to make 'careers open to the talents'.

Printing with movable type, first practised by Gutenberg at Mainz between 1450 and 1460, was, like the growth of grammar schools, an immense aid to the spread of learning. Gutenberg's first major work was the Latin Bible of 1456. An English merchant, William Caxton, who published his first books in Flanders, established a press in Westminster in 1476 and soon found many noble patrons, putting out 100 books in 15 years—18,000 large pages, Chaucer, Malory and Cicero being among the authors he

74

chose. For a long time, however, the price of printed books was too high for there to be big circulations. Paper supplies were not plentiful and the craft of paper-making was slow and laborious.

The universities continued to depend on their libraries of manuscripts for long after the invention of printing. Oxford, for example, had received a magnificent addition, 600 volumes of manuscripts collected by Humphrey, Duke of Gloucester, a brother of Henry V. Collections of printed books took centuries to build up.

Four new colleges were founded at Cambridge and three at Oxford. To take boys from Eton, Henry VI founded King's College, Cambridge, in 1442, giving its provost and fellows larger endowments and more independence than the governing body of any earlier college. Their estates were situated in twenty different counties and their chapel, which Henry VI did not live to see completed, excels in beauty and grandeur that of any other college in the kingdom.

In emulation of her husband Queen Margaret founded another college at Cambridge in 1448 and when she went into exile Edward IV's queen, Elizabeth Woodville, who had

The Divinity School of Oxford University. This splendid example of Perpendicular architecture provided a well-lit spacious room where those seeking degrees could be examined orally and could 'dispute' with the doctors of divinity. The room was used for the interrogation of Archbishop Cranmer when he was a prisoner of Queen Mary I, and for a meeting of Parliament summoned by Charles II

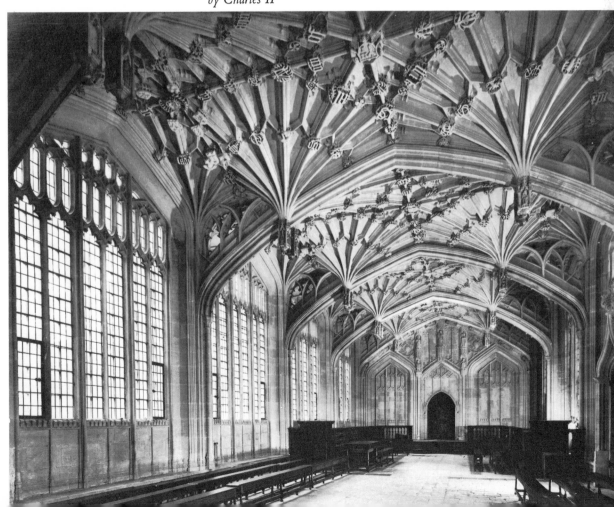

been one of Queen Margaret's ladies-in-waiting, endowed it still further, so that it is called Queens' College in memory of both benefactresses.

The Provost of King's established another college, St Catharine's, in 1473, and in 1497, Jesus College, the last of the medieval foundations, was created by the Bishop of Ely, who used the site of a nunnery that had fallen on bad times and had only two nuns left. The suppression of many minor monasteries and convents in order to use their endowments for new educational purposes was something on which many of the higher clergy were agreed long before the Reformation.

At Oxford the new colleges, Lincoln (1427), All Souls' (1438) and Magdalen (1458), were markedly medieval in conception. The Bishop of Lincoln intended his college to train for work in his vast diocese men who could combat the doctrines of the Lollards. Archbishop Chichele linked with All Souls' a chantry where masses might be said in perpetuity for the souls of those who had died fighting in France. Its chapel, later wrecked by Protestants, was richly adorned with statuary. Magdalen, founded by William Waynflete, Bishop of Winchester and chancellor to Henry VI, was closely modelled on New College (Waynflete had earlier been headmaster of Winchester College before the king made him headmaster of Eton), but it was the first college to provide food and lodging for boys who could pay for them while preparing for their first degrees. Waynflete had to go into hiding on the fall of Henry VI, but later won the approval of both Edward IV and Richard III for the college. He died in 1486, having completed the cloistered quadrangle but not the tall and slender belfry, begun in 1496 and finished in 1505. Over three centuries later Matthew Arnold was thinking of Magdalen when he spoke of Oxford 'whispering from her towers the last enchantments of the Middle Ages'.

The Final Development of Gothic Architecture

In the fifteenth century, when in Italy and France the architects and sculptors of the Renaissance were already taking the temples and palaces of ancient Greece and Rome as their models, England remained attached to the Gothic style, and carried it to a pitch of perfection not attained anywhere else in Europe. Such buildings as the Divinity School at Oxford, St George's Chapel at Windsor, King's College Chapel and, most perfect of all, Henry VII's Chapel at Westminster are witness to the skill and inventiveness of masons.

The fan-vaulted ceilings and enormous windows of these buildings—their walls might almost be said to be made of glass—were by no means exceptional. In cathedrals and parish churches the same energy and creativeness were everywhere apparent and painters of stained glass were often commissioned to take the whole east and west ends of churches for their compositions, making scenes like the Last Judgement or the Crucifixion flow over the whole window, disregarding the delicate division caused by the stone mullions. It is sometimes said that the art of painting and firing stained glass has been lost, but the rich medieval colours and textures now so much admired are partly the result of centuries of weathering. It was not possible until modern times to make glass that was entirely transparent and smooth. Surfaces were slightly rough and even pitted, giving small lichens a lodging and adding to a pictorial beauty which varies with every passing change of cloud and sun outside.

St Botolph, Boston, Lincolnshire, a 15th century church in the Perpendicular style. The belfry, 266 feet high and called Boston Stump, stands beside the estuary of the Witham. Great architectural skill was required to obtain secure foundations in marshy soil for such a weight of stone, an invaluable landmark for sailors trading in and out of this prosperous wool port

Henry VII's Chapel, Westminster Abbey. This Lady Chapel, probably designed by Robert Vertue, and according to Henry's order 'painted garnished and adorned in a goodly and rich a manner as to a king's work apperteyneth', was begun in 1502 and finished in 1512. It contains the tombs of the King and his mother, the work of Peter Torrigiano. The banners belong to Knights of the Order of the Bath. One of the windows commemorates the men of the RAF who lost their lives in the Battle of Britain. It is designed by Hugh Easton and executed by Geoffrey and Anthony Harper

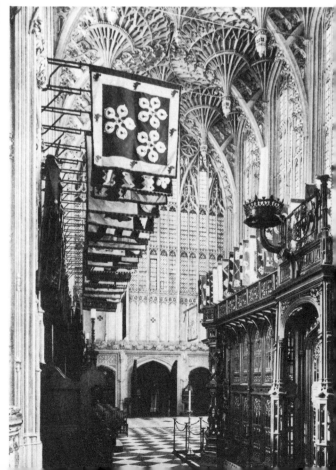

CHAPTER EIGHT

The Sixteenth Century

The Monarchy

England		Scotland	
Henry VII	1485–1509	James IV	1488–1513
Henry VIII	1509–1547	James V	1513–1542
Edward VI	1547–1553	*Mary	1542–1567
Mary I	1553–1558	James VI	1567–1625
Elizabeth I	1558–1603		

* Deposed

James IV of Scotland and the Battle of Flodden

James IV, like his contemporary Henry VIII, quickly won popular admiration for his many outstanding gifts. He succeeded to the throne at the age of fifteen, was an excellent musician and linguist, quick to appreciate what the Renaissance meant in art and scholarship. His subjects seem to have had no objection to his ostentatious style of living and the flaunting of his numerous mistresses. Erasmus of Rotterdam, whom he chose as tutor to one of his many illegitimate children, spoke of his 'wonderful force of intellect and incredible knowledge of all things'. Ambitious to be the first king to tame the savage Highland clans, he learnt to speak Gaelic. Hostile at first to Henry VII, in 1501 he agreed to marry Henry's twelve-year-old daughter, Margaret Tudor, whom the poet William Dunbar welcomed to Scotland in the poem *The Thistle and the Rose*. A third university was established at Aberdeen; in Edinburgh Scotland's first printing press was set up in 1507; and a new Act of Parliament required the eldest sons of barons and freeholders to attend grammar school from the age of eight until they were well grounded in Latin, and thereafter to study 'art and law' for a further three years. This Act expressed no more than good intentions, but had notable influence.

In his thirties, however, James became avid for military glory. He built warships of unprecedented size and provided his soldiers and sailors with the newest and best guns. The fatal alliance with France was renewed, and, against the advice of his best counsellors, he led a splendid army across the Tweed. Henry VIII, who was campaigning in France, had charged the Earl of Surrey with the defence of the border, where he feared an attack, having treated James with contempt. The earl had collected a large force, and the Scots, having allowed him to perform the most daring manoeuvres without interference, abandoned a strong position on Flodden Edge, where their guns and eighteen-foot spears would have been most effective, charged over rough ground and found their spears unwieldy against the deadly eight-foot bills of the English. James was killed in action and with him died nine earls, thirteen lords, hundreds of young noblemen, and thousands of common soldiers. All Scotland was in mourning, but no invasion followed; the English, though their losses had been slight, were not strong enough to attempt one.

The Reformation in England

Ever since the first century Christians have regarded the Bible as the basis of their faith and practice, and the Reformation drew its inspiration from the study, stimulated by the Renaissance, of the oldest surviving manuscripts of the Bible in Greek. The scholars who set out to revise the text were not aware of the obstacles that lay ahead. They had no means of judging the extent of those linguistic changes that had occurred in the five hundred years that separated the Greek spoken by Plato, Aristotle and other classical Greek authors and that used by St Luke and St Paul. Only in the twentieth century has the discovery of casual letters and business documents, written in New Testament times, revealed the contemporary force of words used in the Bible. In Henry VIII's reign, for example, translators were unsure how to render the Lord's Prayer. One wrote: 'Forgive us our trespasses as we forgive those who trespass against us'; another: 'Forgive us our debts as we forgive our debtors'; whereas the scholars of 1961 have put: 'Forgive us the wrong we have done, as we have forgiven those who have wronged us'. From such linguistic causes a host of misunderstandings and misinterpretations arose, separating one Christian sect from another. Some reformers, for example, translated the Greek word *presbyteros*, used in the New Testament to mean an official of the early Church, as 'elder', and this was held to justify a new method of Church government by elected laymen, not ordained priests or ministers. This found favour in Geneva and Scotland, but not in England. Even so outspoken a Protestant as the poet Milton (1608-1674) remarked: 'New presbyter is but old priest writ large.'

Reform and Bible translation went forward together both in England and Germany. Erasmus of Rotterdam (1466-1536), who was Professor of Greek and Lady Margaret Professor of Divinity at Cambridge between 1511 and 1514, produced in 1516 a new Latin version of the New Testament, printed side by side with the Greek text. In his preface he wrote:

> I totally disagree with those who are unwilling that the Holy Scriptures, translated into the common tongue should be read by the unlearned. Christ desires His mysteries to be published abroad as widely as possible . . . and I would that they were translated into all the languages of all Christian people. I wish that the farm worker might sing parts of them at the plough, that the weaver might hum them at the shuttle and that the traveller might beguile the weariness of the way by reciting them.

Soon after Erasmus's departure an Oxford scholar, William Tyndale, arrived in Cambridge to study Greek, and, talking to a learned man who pointed out the dangers of making Bible studies known to unlearned men, he declared, echoing the words of

The fyrst boke

of Moses called Genesis

The fyrst Chapiter.

IN the begynnynge God created heaven and erth. The erth was voyde and emptie/ ād darcknesse was vpon the depe / and the spirite of god moved vpon the water

Than God sayd: let there be lyghte and there was lyghte. And God sawe the lyghte that it was good: ꝗ devyded the lyghte from the darcknesse/and called the lyghte daye /and the darcknesse nyghte: and so of the evenynge and mornynge was made the fyrst daye

And God sayd : let there be a fyrmament betwene the waters/ād let it devyde the waters a sonder. Than God made the fyrmament and parted the waters which were vnder the fyrmament/from the waters that were aboue the fyrmament: And it was so. And God called the fyrmament heaven/And so of the evenynge and morninge was made the seconde daye

And God sayd/let the waters that are vnder heaven gather them selves vnto one place/ that the drye londe may appere: And it came so to passe. And god called the drye londe the erth and the gatherynge togyther of waters called he the see. And God sawe that it was good

B i.

The story of the Creation in Tyndale's translation of the Bible. His poetic choice of words and beautiful rhythms were adopted by the authors of King James's Authorised Version over seventy years later

Erasmus: 'If God spare my life, ere many years I will cause a boy that driveth the plough shall know more of the Scripture than thou dost.' It was not possible for him, however, to pursue this ambition in England, where both Henry VIII and his chief minister, Cardinal Wolsey, were oblivious to the need for reform. The cardinal in fact greatly increased hostility to the Church by his exploitation of the old custom of taking revenues from many different Church appointments for which he did no work, by his extravagant building of palaces like Hampton Court, and by the general ostentation of his life and manners.

The collection of Papal dues also caused resentment both in Germany and Britain. The Popes had planned a new Renaissance church on the site of St Peter's in Rome, a magnificent building, now admired throughout the world, but one which seemed to reformers to be overwhelming proof that the worldliness which they saw in their own churches stemmed from the Papacy itself. Tyndale earned the hatred of those opposed to reform by inserting a criticism of the Pope among the notes in the margin of his translation. On *Exodus*, chapter 35, verse 35, where the people are asked not to bring any more offerings for the building of the tabernacle, because they have already contributed more than enough, he wrote: 'When will the Pope say "Hoo! (Hold!)"

and forbid an offering for the building of St Peter's Church?' By 1530 printed copies of Tyndale's Bible were being smuggled into England and Scotland in considerable numbers; Wolsey had fallen from power and his successor as chancellor, Sir Thomas More, though sympathetic to reform and a close friend of Erasmus, was a severe critic of Tyndale's translation. Both he and Erasmus were aware that reform, if carried out too rapidly, could lead to revolution and war—as it did—and from that their gentle spirits shrank. They had no wish to see the supra-national organisation of the Church destroyed.

Between 1520 and 1530 Germany led the Reformation in Europe and reformers in England followed the dramatic career of Martin Luther, a former Augustinian monk, with growing sympathy. The old 'White Horse Inn' hidden in a dark Cambridge alley became known as 'Germany' because university men used it as a secret meeting place where they could study Lutheranism and exchange copies of books publicly burned as heretical by order of Cardinal Wolsey. A number of the first Protestant martyrs were Cambridge men. Bilney of Trinity Hall was burned at the stake in 1531, Frith of King's in 1533, and William Tyndale in 1536 at Vilvorde in the Netherlands. John Rogers of Pembroke was the first to suffer under Queen Mary.

Of all the Cambridge converts to Protestantism none was more influential than Thomas Cranmer, who was a fellow of Jesus College. In 1531 he was asked to advise Henry VIII about possible grounds for divorcing the Queen, Catherine, daughter of King Ferdinand of Aragon and Queen Isabella of Spain. Papal consent for setting aside this marriage could not be obtained since the Pope wished to avoid a quarrel with the Queen's nephew, Charles V, who had become head of the Holy Roman Empire, as well as king of all the Spanish dominions in Europe and America. Henry noted, however, that the Reformation had undermined the power of Charles V in Germany, where several princes, eager for independence, were supporting Martin Luther, and Cranmer, as one of a party of envoys sent by the king to the court of Charles V, made contact with them. He greatly admired a new Lutheran form for the Mass that he heard in Nuremburg. On his return he was appointed Archbishop of Canterbury; sat in judgement on the king's marriage to Catherine of Aragon, which he declared null and void; and officiated at his wedding to Anne Boleyn in January 1533. In September he baptised their first-born child, Elizabeth.

The break between Henry VIII and Pope Clement VII, who had forbidden him to marry Anne Boleyn, was made final by a series of Acts of Parliament. These were brought in on the advice of Thomas Cromwell, the son of a Putney blacksmith who had risen high in the service of Cardinal Wolsey, and after 1532 became Henry VIII's chief minister. He was an administrator of genius and the Reformation in England on its political and economic side was his work. His ultimate aim was to make Henry Supreme Head of the English Church, but he did this gradually. A first step was to make it illegal for any of the king's subjects to appeal to Rome against decisions by ecclesiastical courts in England. To obtain consent for a series of anti-Papal acts he transformed the Parliament called in 1529 and its methods of conducting its affairs. Previously Parliament had rarely sat for more than a year, and this prolongation from 1529 to 1536 enabled members, through long acquaintance with each other, to acquire a corporate feeling which made their approval or disapproval of any measure proposed by the government a matter of public knowledge and, on occasions, great political importance. This was something new, as foreign ambassadors noted at the time. Cromwell developed the art of lobbying members and influencing their opinion by massive accumulations of facts supporting the government's views. Almost the only opposition he met was from Sir Thomas More and John Fisher, the Bishop of Rochester. They refused on conscientious grounds to show public approval for the king's assumption of complete power over the Church, but the king, though often talking about his own tender conscience, found their objections infuriating, and they, after long imprisonment, interrogation and trial by judges constantly intimidated, were found guilty of treason and publicly executed. Luther's comment was: 'Junker Henry means to be God.'

Between 1536 and 1540 two more Parliaments were elected, composed as before mainly of country gentry with little interest in religious reform. For them the affairs of the Papacy were remote and foreign, and, when the government attacked the religious

Tintern Abbey, Monmouthshire. This Cistercian house, one of the first founded by the order in Britain, lay in a remote part of the Wye valley. Its beautiful 13th century church fell into ruins following the dissolution of the monasteries in Henry VIII's reign

orders as being vehicles for Papal influence in Britain, they readily gave consent to the Acts under which the communities were dissolved and their buildings and estates confiscated. They gave little thought of the consequences to the religious and cultural life of the nation. Later, when the king sold off monastic property, Catholics bought it as well as Protestants.

Cromwell's commissioners, riding from shire to shire, calling at one doomed monastery after another, could scarcely fail to get the evidence their master desired. If a religious house were ill-kept and miserable, it was described as maladministered; if prosperous and hospitable, as forgetful of the vow of poverty. Only in the north did this government inquest spark off a series of rebellions generally called the Pilgrimage of Grace. There the monasteries were still popular, especially for their work in relieving poverty. The rebels voiced different discontents; in the autumn of 1536 a brief rising in Lincolnshire led to the main outbreak in Yorkshire and others in the Lake district. The Yorkshire rebellion was put down by a royal army, over two hundred humble folk being hanged.

In the south and west, where the religious orders held numerous estates in every county, the transfer of property went through smoothly. The size of monastic buildings and churches had always been very large in proportion to the number of men and women under vows. The Benedictines, Augustinians and Cistercians each had over a hundred houses scattered throughout the kingdom, but even the Benedictines of Westminster Abbey, whose foundation dated back six hundred years, numbered no more than sixty monks at the height of their prosperity. Two abbots who opposed the dissolution were executed. Some monks were given small pensions or became parish priests; others disappeared into private life. Only two of the Benedictine monks who had been at Westminster in 1539 returned when a community of twelve was for a time re-constituted there under Queen Mary. In addition to the many hardships caused to the monks and those who depended on them, the nation suffered the loss of an immense part of its artistic and architectural heritage through the destruction of buildings and dispersal of altar plate, vestments and libraries. On the other hand English agriculture benefited. The monks had become backward-looking, unadventurous landlords, little interested in increasing the productivity of their estates. The country gentry who bought abbey lands were seldom the greedy and heartless men of popular satire; they were for the most part hard-working and ambitious, often ready, in the spirit of the Renaissance, to experiment with new crops and new methods.

After the dissolution some of the bigger and more unwieldy dioceses were broken up and new Bishops of Oxford, Chester, Gloucester, Bristol and Peterborough were created. The great monastic churches in those towns became cathedrals. At Canterbury, Carlisle, Durham, Ely, Norwich, Rochester, Winchester and Worcester the bishops remained after the monks had dispersed. The medieval cathedrals of the Archbishop of York and the Bishops of Bangor, Chichester, Exeter, Hereford, Lichfield, Lincoln, Llandaff, London (old St Paul's), St Asaph, St David's, Salisbury and Wells had never been attached to monasteries, but together with the former monastic churches were each put under the rule of a Dean and Chapter.

While this reorganisation was going on the reformers received some encouragement from the issue by the king in 1536 of Ten Articles of Religion, largely the work of Cranmer, 'to stablish Christian quietness and unity and to avoid contentious opinions'. Henry was showing a fitful interest in Lutheranism and the Articles were a compromise between old and new to which he attached royal Injunctions imposing them on the clergy. Further Injunctions in 1538 and 1539 made obligatory the provision of Bibles in English in all churches and public readings from them. The translation was essentially that of William Tyndale revised by his friend Miles Coverdale, Bishop of Exeter. Private persons, if not of low birth, were permitted to buy Bibles for reading at home.

After 1540 the king moved back towards 'the old religion', though his personal regard for Cranmer remained intact. Thomas Cromwell, who had brought over from Germany the king's fourth wife, Anne of Cleves, was dismissed and executed. Henry, having quickly divorced Anne, again married into the powerful family of the Duke of Norfolk, choosing Catherine Howard, a cousin of Anne Boleyn, but she proved unfaithful and was put to death in 1542. The next year he married Catherine Parr, a connection of the Neville family. When he died in 1547 the treasury was empty, the coinage debased, and the kingdom divided by religious controversy.

As soon as the king was dead the Earl of Hertford, uncle to the nine-year-old Edward VI, Henry's son by his third wife, Jane Seymour, was made Duke of Somerset and Lord Protector. An idealist without common sense or self-control, he quickly brought in far-reaching religious reforms, including a service book in English called a Book of Common Prayer. Cranmer had long been at work preparing its beautiful paraphrases of the Mass and of many medieval Latin prayers. It also contained precise instructions on the conduct of worship and the vestments to be worn.

The government which ordered the use of the 1549 Prayer Book did not last long. The Duke of Somerset was arrested and executed on the orders of the Duke of Northumberland, who made himself Protector. He too favoured reform and a revised version of the Prayer Book was brought out in 1552. This was again the work of Cranmer and still further influenced by Protestant theology, but the new forms of worship had not had time to become familiar to congregations when in 1553 Edward VI, a delicate boy, died and was succeeded by his half-sister Mary, a fanatical Catholic, determined to restore Papal authority. Many prominent Protestants fled abroad. Some two thousand priests who refused to comply with government decrees were deprived of their livings. It was not surprising that the new government should regard Protestants as potential traitors. The Duke of Northumberland had attempted to substitute a Protestant queen, Lady Jane Grey, for Queen Mary. A Kentish Protestant, Sir Thomas Wyatt, having secretly raised an army of rebels, reached the gates of London before he was arrested. The Government suspected for a time that Princess Elizabeth, Anne Boleyn's daughter, had been involved in this, and although she was spared, Lady Jane Grey was executed. Wyatt and many of his followers were also put to death. The queen at once married Philip, the Catholic heir to the kingdom of Spain.

In 1555 a violent persecution of Protestants began and many were burned at Smithfield, just outside the walls of London, and in other towns. These Protestant martyrs were mostly men and women of humble birth, some of them very young. Two leading reformers, Thomas Cranmer and Hugh Latimer, Bishop of Worcester, were now over seventy. A third, Nicholas Ridley, Bishop of London, was over fifty. Having been dismissed and imprisoned they were burnt at the stake in Oxford. These blows, coming so suddenly, left a deep-seated hatred of continental Catholicism.

Queen Mary's reign was, however, short and under her successor Queen Elizabeth, the 1552 Prayer Book was re-introduced with minor alterations. Its use was not at first enforced and for the next four hundred years bishops had to permit many local variations. Scarcely anywhere was the uniformity enacted by Parliament strictly enforced, but when the danger of invasion by the Catholic power of Spain became imminent, church-going was made a test of loyalty to the queen; those who refused to conform and went to Mass in secret were sometimes fined and, under the stress of war, persecuted. There were a number of high-born Catholics, some of them in court circles, whose loyalty was never in doubt, but others sent their sons abroad to be trained for the priesthood, usually by Jesuits, at Douai, Valladolid and Rome. After ordination they came back in disguise 'to convert England'. If they were caught, they were in the eyes of the law traitors; in their own view, martyrs. Tortured to make them betray the names of Catholics to whom they had secretly administered the Sacraments, they were then convicted of treason and died fearful deaths; 187 priests were executed, 110 of them after the Armada campaign of 1588. Lay people, some of them women, also caught in this tragic dilemma—how to be true to Catholicism without seeming to adhere to the queen's enemies—were put on trial and condemned to death, though not in great numbers.

Catholics were not the only 'nonconformists' to suffer persecution under Queen Elizabeth's government. Among Protestants there were many who were dissatisfied with 'the middle way', and some called Separatists who wished to dispense with a State church. One Separatist, Henry Barrow, was hanged for sedition, and many of his sect fled to Holland. The Puritans, as they were called, a vague term for Protestants who would not accept the forms of worship laid down by law, were politically powerful in the 1580s, but after that quiescent until the next century.

The general praise for Queen Elizabeth's government, which raised England from an abyss of weakness and division to a peak of unity and strength, sometimes obscures the fact that religious minorities were persecuted in her time. What happened was, in comparison with the terrible atrocities perpetrated during the religious wars in France and the Netherlands, a small but black spot on her fame. Politics and religion were still, as in Catholic countries, as much entangled as they had been in medieval times, and not until the eighteenth century was any legal basis for religious tolerance, even for dissident Protestant sects, clearly established. Catholic emancipation was not enacted until 1829.

Renaissance and Reformation in Education

The first boys' school to be touched by the spirit of the Renaissance was St Paul's, founded in London by Dean Colet in 1510. Colet was a merchant's son and a friend of Erasmus, who wrote new textbooks for him and his 153 scholars. These were 'children of all nations and countries indifferently' (a wise provision in a town so cosmopolitan) and were given instruction in Greek as well as Latin free, after payment of an entrance fee of fourpence.

In the hands of less gifted men than Colet his ideals unfortunately became the source of much misery and educational frustration. Ancient Greek and Latin were not the most sensible subjects in which to drill the sons of merchants who left school ignorant of English literature and often of modern languages, history and geography. The pursuit of classical learning and the intellectual prestige attached to it diverted the brains and divided the aspirations of the young for the next four hundred years. It was an odd result to come from a revolt against a Church that had for centuries united the scholars of Europe by using Latin as a living language. No wonder Shakespeare's schoolboy went 'unwillingly' to a place where frequent and hearty birchings were given for failure to memorise the grammar of Cicero or to construe the poetry of Virgil. This evil was self-perpetuating; for centuries the universities produced an excess of men qualified to teach the classics, and the schools had to use them, since those with knowledge of other subjects were not available.

With the destruction of the monasteries, friaries, and chantry chapels the grammar schools attached to them also came to an end. By Edward VI's reign their loss was so much regretted that in some towns, Southampton and Birmingham, for example, new schools were established bearing the king's name. The process continued under Queen Elizabeth, who, in 1560, reconstituted Westminster School. Christ's Hospital grew out of a school for foundlings established under Edward VI in the deserted buildings once owned by the Grey Friars in London.

In Elizabeth's reign new schools were also set up, endowed by rich men: Rugby in 1567, the benefaction of a London grocer; Harrow in 1571, that of a yeoman landowner; Charterhouse of a great financier; and Dulwich College of Edward Alleyn, a successful actor and theatre-owner. At Shrewsbury the municipality founded the school where Sir Philip Sidney was a pupil. In imitation of the Mercers' Company who had been given the management of St Paul's School, the Merchant Taylors founded their school in 1562, and so in various ways the Christian tradition in education survived all the political and economic catastrophies of the century.

The sixteenth century also saw the expansion of the universities. This benefited greatly from the intellectual interests and prowess of the Tudor monarchs. At Oxford Brasenose College was founded in 1509 and Corpus Christi in 1517. The college that Cardinal Wolsey planned as Oxford's rival to King's at Cambridge was re-founded as Christ Church by Henry VIII in 1532, though he did not add to Wolsey's dining hall, kitchens and unfinished quadrangle. Trinity College, Oxford, founded in 1555, was the creation of one of Henry VIII's court officials, Sir Thomas Pope (a Catholic who, during Queen Mary's reign, was put in charge of Princess Elizabeth). He regretted that the study of Greek had fallen into neglect at Eton in his day and so he modelled Trinity statutes on those given by Bishop Foxe to Corpus Christi, directing special attention to Greek and Latin. St John's College was established by a merchant tailor of Reading, Sir Thomas White, who later became Lord Mayor of London and organised resistance to the rebel

Sir Thomas Wyatt. Exeter College was re-founded in 1566, and for Jesus College a Welshman, Hugh Price, was given a charter by the Queen in 1571.

The number of new colleges founded at Cambridge was even more striking—Christ's in 1505, and St John's in 1511, both endowed by Lady Margaret Beaufort, mother of Henry VII; Magdalene in 1542; in 1546 Trinity, a royal foundation rivalling Christ Church in size; in 1557 Gonville and Caius; and in 1584 Emmanuel, of which its Puritan founder, Sir William Mildmay, said to the Queen: 'I have set an acorn which, when it becomes an oak, God alone knows what will be the fruit thereof.' He spoke prophetically, for Emmanuel soon numbered among its undergraduates John Cotton (1584-1652), one of the founders of New England, and John Harvard, who, dying at the age of 31, left a legacy and his library for a new university in America which still bears his name.

The century also saw the making of the first public library in Europe—the Bodleian at Oxford, named after Sir Thomas Bodley, who in 1598 took pity on the university library which stood empty, robbed of its 'popish' books by Edward VI's commissioners. The Bodleian became entitled to a free copy of every new book published in England, but the nucleus of its treasures were the books and manuscripts of a Portuguese Bishop, Jerome Osorius. They had been given to Sir Thomas by the Earl of Essex, Queen Elizabeth's ill-starred favourite. In commanding an assault upon Cadiz in 1596, when a second Armada was fitting out, he had won much glory but little loot, and on the voyage home had stopped at Faro. There, with his 'courtier's, soldier's, scholar's eye, tongue, sword' he had considered the bishop's possessions fair game for a heretical general.

The Reformation in Scotland

The Church in Scotland had developed the same faults as in England but the economy of the country made them more difficult to remedy. The impulse towards reform came from the towns, most of which lay on the east coast, where there was a constant coming and going of students visiting the main centres of the Reformation in Germany and Switzerland. In a country where long winter nights and bad weather held communities together at close quarters there were two pastimes, gossip and fighting, and the new ideas from the continent produced an explosive mixture.

Out of the whole land surface of Scotland with its mountains, moors and lakes only a fifth was cultivable, and of that fifth nearly half was owned by the Church, and so the wealth of the higher clergy was particularly conspicuous. It had moreover corrupted the religious orders more seriously than in other countries.

The first Protestant to suffer death for his opinions was Patrick Hamilton, a young scholar who had studied at Marburg and Geneva and was burnt at the stake in St Andrews in 1528. His fate, however, was exceptional and for the next fourteen years, though there was much persecution, there were few martyrs. By 1542 the English branches of the religious orders had been dissolved and Henry VIII began to interfere in his most megalomaniac way in Scottish affairs. In reply James V attempted an ill-organised invasion along the west coast. This led to defeat at Solway Moss, and soon after the battle James died, leaving his second wife, Mary of Guise, as Regent for their week-old daughter Mary. Her chief supporter was Cardinal Beaton, Archbishop of

Glasgow Cathedral, the only medieval cathedral remaining in use in Scotland

St Andrews, and together they sought military aid from the French in order to defend Scotland against Henry VIII. Temporarily, however, the Protestant party seized power and made a treaty with the English promising that Mary, when she was of age, should marry Henry's son, Edward. The treaty did not stand for long; the Protestants were out-manoeuvred by the cardinal and Mary was crowned Queen of Scots. In a rage Henry offered a reward of £1,000 to anyone who would murder the cardinal, and sent an army into the Lowlands which captured Edinburgh and Leith, burnt the wooden houses and destroyed some of the finest Lowland monasteries, besides many villages. The cardinal's party seized a leading Protestant, George Wishart, on a charge of collaboration with the English, and burnt him at the stake in St Andrews. Soon afterwards a group of Protestant nobles attacked Cardinal Beaton in his own castle, stabbed him to death, and flung his body out of a window. With the assassins was a young black-bearded priest named John Knox, recently converted to Protestantism, who afterwards wrote a history of his times in which he declared it was God's will that the cardinal, Wishart's judge, should die. From such claims by individuals to have personal knowledge of God came much of the evil as well as the good of the Reformation. Knox with the assassins was besieged in the castle of St Andrews by a French force. Promised help from England did not arrive, and they surrendered. Knox with other prisoners was made a galley slave. Later the same year an English force sent by Protector Somerset defeated the forces of the Queen Mother, Mary of Guise, at Pinkie on the Esk.

After two years the French released Knox. He came to England, was appointed chaplain to Edward VI and was one of the first to use the 1552 Book of Common Prayer. On the accession of Mary Tudor he took refuge on the continent and was attracted, like thousands of other Protestant refugees, to Geneva, where John Calvin (1509-1564) was laying the foundations of Protestant teaching and practice in what the reformers had made an independent city state. To demonstrate their ideas they set up a regime more strict than anything ever conceived in Rome. Churchgoing was compulsory; the central part of every service was the sermon; psalms and hymns were unaccompanied; for such misdemeanours as singing a profane song the church elders demanded penance in front of the congregation; for adultery the punishment was death. Yet for the Protestant world Geneva became the 'Holy City' to which ministers came for training and went forth to convert the world.

Knox returned to Scotland in 1555, and at once began preaching sermons attacking the Queen Mother for failing to reform the Church. The next year he decided to return to Geneva for a time, but the example he left behind inspired a powerful group of nobles calling themselves Lords of the Congregation to draw up a document called the First Covenant. To this signatures were obtained from all over Scotland; it proposed 'to establish the most blessed Word of God' and 'to forsake and renounce the congregation of Satan'—in other words, to break with Rome and set up a reformed Church which should hold services in the vernacular on the lines of the new English Book of Common Prayer.

The Catholic party had sent the young Queen of Scots to France for safety and in April 1558 she was married in Paris to Francis, heir to the French throne. The King of France, Henry II, who had been a persecutor of French Protestants, proclaimed Mary Queen of England, Scotland and Ireland. If the French regarded Elizabeth as a usurper, the Scottish Protestants felt themselves to be in danger. Knox returned and his preaching aroused frantic enthusiasm. There were riots in St Andrews, Leith, Stirling and other places. Mobs desecrated churches and smashed altars, pictures and statues. Fear of French interference increased in July when Henry II died and Francis and Mary succeeded him.

Queen Elizabeth, young in age but already old in statecraft, realised that if the Protestant cause in Scotland were to fail, England would be in danger of simultaneous attack across the Channel and the northern border. Yet she disliked helping rebels against their anointed queen, and, to make matters worse, Knox, with Mary of Guise in mind, had published a book entitled *The First Blast of the Trumpet against the Monstrous Regiment of Women*. In this he stated with his usual lack of tact that 'to promote a woman to bear rule, superiority, dominion or empire above any realm, nation or city is repugnant to Nature; is contumely to God'. When in 1560 Mary of Guise died, Queen Elizabeth quietly negotiated at Berwick a treaty by which she promised to send military aid to the Scottish Protestants if they were in need, provided that they assisted

John Knox's House, Edinburgh. Knox was minister at St Giles' Church from 1561 to 1572 and it is believed that the house in the centre of the picture, built in 1490, is where he then lived

her in the event of a French attack. There was no word in the treaty about a religious settlement, yet it laid the foundation for the future union of England and Scotland.

In the absence of Mary, the Scottish Protestant leaders could not call together a Parliament, but they quickly assembled 'the Estates of the Realm', sometimes called the Reformation Parliament, consisting of about a hundred fervent Protestants. They at once established a national church on Presbyterian lines, ruled by Kirk Sessions of lay elders, who possessed the power to ordain ministers. The General Assembly of this new Kirk of Scotland, meeting once or twice a year, soon became a body where many secular as well as ecclesiastical matters were debated. Christmas and Easter were no longer observed; Knox's liturgy was abandoned in favour of extemporisation; and Holy Communion, which he intended to be the centre of religious life, was celebrated less and less often.

In 1561 Mary Queen of Scots, widowed at the age of nineteen after less than a year on the throne of France, returned to a new Scotland where all power lay with a Protestant nobility backed by Protestant mobs, yet for four years her wit and beauty and the lavish splendour of her court won her great popularity. Everybody expected her to marry again and many suitors were proposed. From England Queen Elizabeth sent a Catholic nobleman, Henry Stuart, Lord Darnley, an unintelligent youth of nineteen, yet she for some strange reason fell in love, and married him in 1565. When he proved to be a debauchee, she began to rely more and more on her Italian secretary Riccio. Darnley, madly jealous, one day entered her room while Riccio was there, and held her in her chair while his companions took Riccio out and stabbed him to death. Mary was six months' pregnant and the murderers may have hoped for a fatal miscarriage, leaving Darnley as king. Mary now hated her husband and so nearly a year later, when his enemies blew his house up with gunpowder and left his strangled body naked in the garden, suspicion fell on her. Isolated and bewildered, she turned to a charming and reckless Protestant, James Hepburn fourth Earl of Bothwell, who had befriended her mother. Three months after Darnley's death she married him according to Protestant rites in Edinburgh. This alienated both Catholics and Protestants, and Bothwell's enemies forced the queen to abdicate in favour of her baby son by Darnley, who was proclaimed James VI in 1567. He was brought up in the Protestant faith and never saw his mother again. After two months in prison Mary escaped and took refuge in England. There, to her surprise, Elizabeth, whose letters had once seemed so friendly, not only refused to meet her but actually kept her under close guard for seventeen years, moving her from one isolated castle to another. Even this did not quell Mary's proud spirit; she never abandoned hope of recovering her freedom, but in 1587, the year before the Armada sailed, letters passing between Mary and Catholic conspirators were intercepted by Elizabeth's Council, and Mary was put on trial and executed. She was forty-four years old.

Ocean Trade and Naval Strength

In medieval times kings had no regular navy, and Henry VIII has been called the father of the Royal Navy because he spent lavishly on building ships designed solely for fighting, instead of restricting himself to the requisition of merchant vessels, as his predecessors had done. He also brought craftsmen from the Netherlands to create naval arsenals where heavy guns and gunpowder could be manufactured. Great technical progress was achieved with artillery—heavy guns were put in the waist of ships and fired from gun ports. Light guns continued to be mounted on the high decks, or 'castles' at the stern and bows, but gradually broadside firing produced a revolution in naval tactics. This in turn meant that harbours had to be protected and new forts, like Hurst Castle on the Solent, built to accommodate guns capable of defending them. Old castles had no platforms big enough to allow for recoil after firing; the new were

Guns at Walmer Castle, Kent. One of the coastal forts built by Henry VIII in 1539 to accommodate his new artillery. The castle later became the official residence of the Lord Warden of the Cinque Ports. William Pitt the Younger, after resigning the premiership in 1801, lived here in retirement and organised local defence forces against Napoleon's intended invasion. The fine gardens were laid out by his niece, Lady Hester Stanhope

specially designed with round towers giving a wide circle of fire and presenting low profiles to the guns of enemy ships.

Such coastal defences were expensive, and so was the maintenance of the new warships. Sails, ropes, wooden hulls and iron fittings deteriorated, being constantly exposed to the salt in the wind and waves and encrustations of weed and shell fish. Crews too suffered from the Government's constant shortage of funds, being ill-fed and irregularly paid.

At sea the old methods by which men without mechanical aids 'smelt their way' through rain, storm and fog, tide-race and shoal, were seen to be both slow and dangerous. William Bourne, a surveyor and gunner of Gravesend, published in 1571 a *Manual of the Art of Navigation* which showed in simple practical terms how mathematics and geometry could bring merchant captains swiftly to port ahead of their market rivals and even save their lives in bad weather. A copy soon became part of the equipment of every ship sailing to unfamiliar waters. Further help came from Dr John Dee, a much-travelled scholar and a friend of continental astronomers, who wrote a splendidly clear introduction to a new edition of Euclid's *Elements*, explaining how essential they were to a sailor's needs. Later, as a reward for his mathematical work, Sir Walter Raleigh introduced him to the queen, who had to protect him against a charge of witchcraft.

The risks attending ocean voyages were none the less omnipresent and to spread their impact a number of joint-stock companies were formed in London and in the west country to develop the new trade routes. The expeditions they financed were conducted with great boldness and courage. Three well-equipped ships, sent out by a London company 'for the Discovery of Unknown Lands', began a search for a north-east passage to India. They sailed to the North Cape of Norway in 1553, but were scattered by a storm. Their leader, Sir Hugh Willoughby, died with his crew, caught in winter ice. A second ship disappeared, but the third, under Richard Chancellor, made port on the White Sea coast. Chancellor landed and travelled to Moscow, where the Tsar Ivan the Terrible (1530-1584) received him kindly. The information he obtained encouraged his

Map engraved by Hondius in 1590, probably in London. It shows by a continuous line the circumnavigation of Drake (1577-1588) and by a dotted line that of Cavendish (1586-1588). The land mass marked 'Terra Australis was conjectured; Dutch sailors of the 17th century were the first to encounter the west coast of Australia; the east coast was discovered a century later by Captain James Cook, who also circumnavigated Antarctica

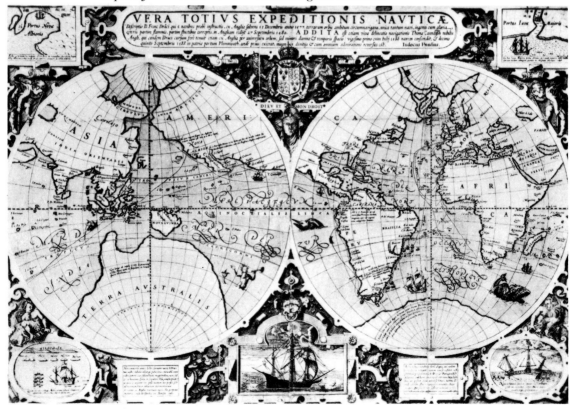

backers in London to start trading with Russia, and they became known as the Muscovy Company.

The search for a north-west passage continued, inspired by the writings of Sir Humphrey Gilbert, a Devon man related to Sir Walter Raleigh, and aided by new methods of navigation. In the 1570s Martin Frobisher, and in the 1580s John Davis, explored large parts of the north-west coast of Canada. In 1577 the Devon sailor Francis Drake set out in the *Pelican*, later renamed the *Golden Hind*, on the first voyage round the world to be undertaken by an Englishman. He made first for the straits of Magellan and then robbed the Spaniards in South American waters, stuffing his 75-foot ship with treasure. On his way home he searched in vain for a western outlet to the supposed north-west passage, and, crossing the Pacific to the Moluccas, took on the first English sea-borne consignment of those oriental spices on which the overseas empire of the Portuguese had been founded.

Four years after Drake's return another Devon man, Sir Walter Raleigh, one of the most gifted and mysterious figures at Queen Elizabeth's court, organised the first of three expeditions to the North American coast, choosing the warm latitudes of what later became the colonies of Virginia and Carolina. Parties of over a hundred were put on shore; one of these was visited in 1587 by Sir Francis Drake, and fearful that the Spanish Armada might destroy their homeland, returned with him. Those who remained disappeared, but not before they had sent home a mass of scientific information such as Raleigh demanded—beautiful illustrations by the artist John White of the life of the Indian tribes, and details of soil, climate and crops. In 1588 Raleigh was busy raising land forces to resist the Spanish troops that the admiral of the Armada intended to bring across from the Netherlands. The new warship he had built, the *Ark Royal*, he had sold to the government, and her commander, Lord Admiral Howard, wrote to Lord Burghley in February, 1588, after taking her on patrol: 'I pray you tell her Majesty from me that her money was well given for the Ark Raleigh, for I think her the odd ship in the world for all conditions . . . there can be no great ship make me change and go out of her.'

It is not known what improvements Raleigh had incorporated in this ship to win such a eulogy, but his retentive brain and ready pen had noted all the new skills and knowledge of the sea that ocean trade had brought—even such simple things as how many times a ship's length in anchor cable to pay out for safe riding in a roadstead or harbour.

The long-threatened dispatch of the Armada in the summer of 1588, the thirtieth year of Elizabeth's reign, put the whole organising power of her government on sea and land to the test, for this was to be an amphibious invasion involving the seizure of a Channel port and the transport of an army from the Netherlands. The rebel provinces of the Spanish Netherlands, those to the north of the mouth of the Rhine, had not been subdued and the Duke of Parma was reluctant to obey the orders of King Philip to embark for a campaign in England. The 'invincible Armada' included ships from Portugal and Florence and the Spaniards proved incapable of supplying this fleet with sufficient food, water, guns and ammunition. Drake had destroyed thirty-seven ships in Cadiz harbour the year before and burnt thousands of barrels needed for ships' stores of water. There were about 20,000 soldiers and only 10,000 sailors on board the Armada's one hundred and thirty ships and many were on short rations before they sighted the Lizard. From lack of wind the Spaniards had a slow passage up the Channel. Though harassed, they lost only two ships; an explosion on board one and collision damage to another led to the capture of both. Off Calais the Spanish Admiral ordered his ships to anchor. An attack by English fireships at night caused a panic flight before a rising wind which nearly drove the whole fleet ashore, and then by a sudden shift scattered it over the North Sea, preventing the admiral from remustering. He and a little over half of his ships reached Spain by way of Scotland and Ireland. About forty were wrecked; some crews landed in Scotland or Ireland and were taken prisoner; others were massacred; and many died of thirst and starvation. For more than a month neither Queen Elizabeth nor Philip of Spain knew what had happened. Raleigh wrote: 'They (the enemy) were all sent back again to their countries to witness and recount the worthy achievements of their invincible and terrible navy—with all so great and terrible an ostentation, they did not in all their sailing round about England so much as sink or take one ship, bark, pinnace or cockboat of ours, or ever burned one sheepcote of this land.'

The Spaniards were still feared in England, though needlessly. Their great empire with its long lines of communication was no menace; instead of encouraging trade between Spanish America and the rest of Europe they had sought a monopoly, and by pursuing a senseless quarrel with the small 'heretic' nations of England and the Netherlands had undermined the Portuguese empire in Asia, as the English and Dutch were quick to see. James Lancaster led an expedition to Ceylon and Malacca in 1595. Will Adams became the first Englishman to reach Japan and make friends among the ruling class there. In 1600 the East India Company was formed and the next year Lancaster took five ships to Java, an adventure to be followed by over two centuries of enterprise and growing sea-borne trade with the Far East. The monopoly granted to the Company was sensible in the circumstances when a concentration of knowledge, capital and government protection was essential for success. When Elizabeth died her subjects had founded no colonies overseas, but were in all respects prepared to do so, confident that English seamen were second to none.

The Rise of the English Theatre

The public performance of plays on Biblical and mythological subjects had been a feature of saints' days and festivals long before Tudor times and belonged to a tradition damaged, but not destroyed, by the Reformation. The texts of 'mystery' plays enacted at Chester, Coventry and Wakefield have survived, and the various scenes are taken by the crafts or 'mysteries' appropriate to them—the bakers played the Last Supper, and taverners the Marriage Feast at Cana. In York and Newcastle, Noah and the Flood was played by the shipbuilders, at Chester by the waterleaders (conduit-builders) and water drawers of the river Dee. Audiences were much attached to stage business—they loved Noah to be the hen-pecked husband—and liked realistic effects—at Coventry the drapers provided a Mouth of Hell that 'burned and harmed none'.

In Tudor times plays came into demand among the nobility, who had abandoned their cold ill-lit castles and moved into country mansions, often built of brick with southern facades which were almost walls of glass. Such houses were not only family homes but centres of rural industry for miles around, housing retinues of servants and workpeople engaged in making cream and butter, baking bread, brewing ale, growing fruit, vegetables, herbs and spices, preparing meat, fish and poultry obtained from local sources and many other kinds of work, all done on a communal basis. Wages were low but board and lodging were free. It was a happy time, people of all classes mixing freely. Sometimes a country house would entertain the queen on one of her 'progresses' and then fetes and shows were the order of the day. Possibly Shakespeare's first boyhood sight of a play was when Elizabeth arrived at Kenilworth Castle, near Stratford-on-Avon, which she had given to her favourite, Robert Dudley, Earl of Leicester. There in the great hall built by John of Gaunt two centuries before there were plays and dancing throughout her stay.

Before 1576, when the first theatre was constructed, there had been no building in England specially designed for drama. If troupes could not perform in the dining hall of some noble house or university college the rectangular courtyard of an inn sufficed. After the Reformation the deserted hall of the Black Friars in London became a play-house. A circular building, Shakespeare's 'wooden O', was a great improvement on a rectangular auditorium. In front of the two-tier stage which jutted out into the centre of the theatre stood 'the groundlings' and, high above them in the surrounding galleries, were those of 'the better sort', a mixed gathering of courtiers, merchants and tradesmen, standing or sitting on stools and protected by the roof from any passing shower.

The standard of writing and acting generally provided may be gathered from the Prince's sarcastic remarks to the strolling players in *Hamlet*, which are thought to refer to Edward Alleyn's company, or from the proud words of Christopher Marlowe's prologue to *Tamburlaine*:

> *From jigging veins of rhyming mother wits,*
> *And such conceits as clownage keeps in pay,*
> *We'll lead you to the stately tent of war,*
> *Where you shall hear the Scythian Tamburlaine*
> *Threatening the world with high astounding terms,*
> *And scourging kingdoms with his conquering sword.*

Women's parts were all played by boys from choir schools where they had been taken for the beauty of their unbroken voices. These singers were hired out to the theatres because social custom did not allow women to display themselves on the stage. The versatility of the boys, who were trained to play women of widely different age and rank, constantly delighted Elizabethan audiences.

The queen and her courtiers often asked the players to perform at court and protected them from the hostility of Puritans, who regarded players as servants of Satan. No one doubted the power of the spoken word for good or evil. Elizabeth, towards the end of her life, noted how popular *Richard II* was, and realising what doubts there were about the succession to her own throne, said: 'Know you not I am Richard II?'

House of Tudor and Stuart:
The Tudor and Stuart Succession

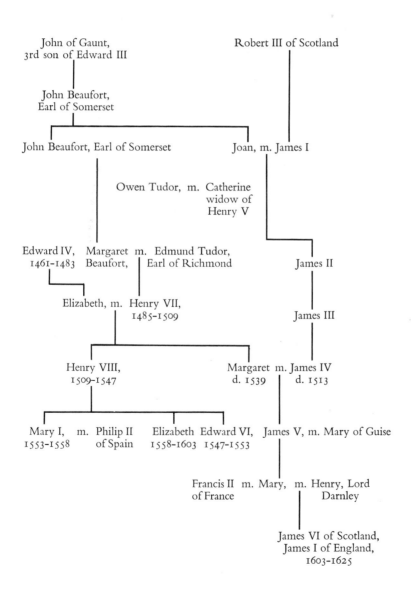

John of Gaunt,
3rd son of Edward III

Robert III of Scotland

John Beaufort,
Earl of Somerset

John Beaufort, Earl of Somerset

Joan, m. James I

Owen Tudor, m. Catherine
widow of
Henry V

Edward IV,   Margaret m. Edmund Tudor,
1461-1483   Beaufort,   Earl of Richmond

James II

Elizabeth, m. Henry VII,
1485-1509

James III

Henry VIII,
1509-1547

Margaret m. James IV
d. 1539   d. 1513

Mary I,   m. Philip II   Elizabeth Edward VI, James V, m. Mary of Guise
1553-1558   of Spain   1558-1603 1547-1553

Francis II m. Mary, m. Henry, Lord
of France   Darnley

James VI of Scotland,
James I of England,
1603-1625

97

The House of Stuart and Hanoverian Succession

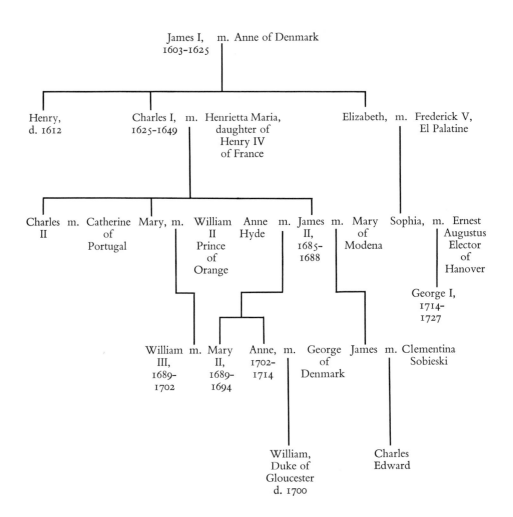

James I,   m. Anne of Denmark
1603–1625

Henry,   Charles I,   m. Henrietta Maria,   Elizabeth, m. Frederick V,
d. 1612   1625–1649   daughter of   El Palatine
                               Henry IV
                               of France

Charles m. Catherine   Mary, m.   William   Anne   m. James   m. Mary   Sophia, m. Ernest
II   of   II   Hyde   II,   of   Augustus
            Portugal   Prince of   1685–   Modena   Elector
                                  Orange   1688   of
                                                                                      Hanover

                                                                                   George I,
                                                                                   1714–
                                                                                   1727

          William m. Mary   Anne, m. George   James m. Clementina
          III,   II,   1702–   of   Sobieski
          1689–   1689–   1714   Denmark
          1702   1694

                    William,   Charles
                    Duke of   Edward
                    Gloucester
                    d. 1700

CHAPTER NINE

The Seventeenth Century

The Monarchy

England   *Scotland*
Elizabeth I 1558–1603   James VI 1567–1603

The United Kingdom

James VI & I	1603–1625
Charles I	1625–1649
The Commonwealth	1649–1660
Charles II	1660–1685
James II	1685–1688
William III & Mary II	1689–1694
William III	1694–1702

The Disunited Kingdom

To mark the union of the crowns of Scotland and England a new ensign was invented—the red cross of St George was superimposed on the white cross of St Andrew. The opportunity of putting an end to centuries of discord had fallen to James I, a man who, in spite of all his sincere desire to promote peace and prosperity, was what his great contemporary, Henry IV of France called him, 'the wisest fool in Christendom'.

Experience of kingship in Scotland, a country he understood but did not love, was a disadvantage in England, a country he loved but did not understand. He adhered to the Tudor view that government should relieve unemployment and promote new industries, and in his reign Scotland and Ireland as well as England prospered economically.

Yet it was in Scotland and Ireland that James sowed the seeds of the civil war that was to bring his son Charles to the scaffold. He had never liked the Presbyterian customs of the Scottish Church and by a mixture of bullying and persuasion tried to bring its practices into line with those of England. He met with passive resistance. Charles I treated the Scots with even less sympathy and commonsense, and the quarrel continued.

In Ireland James determined that the Six Counties in the north, Tyrone, Coleraine, Donegal, Fermanagh, Armagh and Cavan, should be 'planted', that is colonised, with Protestants from Scotland. As the native Irish were Catholics and their devotion to the Church had been increased since the Reformation by Jesuit missions, those planted

(left) The Lyte Jewel. Thomas Lyte presented James I with an elaborate family tree, the result of much research into the origins of the Stuart family. The king was so delighted that in return he sent this miniature portrait of himself in a gold pendant enamelled and set with diamonds; (below) a torn page in the Journal of the House of Commons, 1621. A marginal note says: 'King James in Council with his own hand rent out the Protestation.' The motion which offended the king stated: 'In the handling of the business of the State, every member of this House hath, and of right ought to have, freedom of speech to propound, treat and reason about the same.'

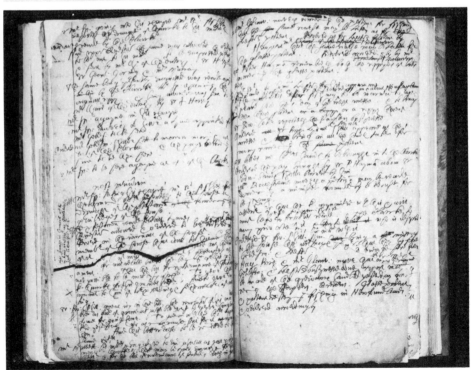

were unpopular, though too few in number to do more than irritate the Irish and add to the general confusion into which the country fell.

It was not until 1636, when Charles I appointed Thomas Wentworth, later Earl of Strafford, Lord Deputy of Ireland, that the future of the island was damaged beyond repair. Wentworth had been a youthful member of the House of Commons where he shone as a critic of the government. Now he had adopted the view that only absolute monarchy could meet the kingdom's needs. Like Charles, whose entire confidence he possessed, he was temperamentally unfit to govern, yet filled with the conceit that he could. His intelligence and energy were enormous; he found Ireland divided in religion, politics and social life, and her sea coasts infested with pirates. In five years he managed at no great financial cost to get rid of the pirates and bring a semblance of order and efficiency into the government. In the process, however, he offended, and often humiliated, every section of the population, and when he was recalled in the autumn of 1639, news from England convinced the Irish Catholics that Charles's government must soon fall, as it had already done in Scotland.

A year earlier the Assembly of the Church of Scotland had proclaimed the deposition of all the Scottish bishops and the rejection of the English Book of Common Prayer. Rebellion, organised by the Covenanters, headed by James Graham, Marquis of Montrose, and Archibald Campbell, eighth Earl of Argyll, caused Charles I to move to the border with a large but ill-disciplined force, only to find himself facing an army of battle-hardened Scottish mercenaries recently returned from the continent, led by Alexander Leslie, who had taken command of the Protestant armies in Germany when Gustavus Adolphus, King of Sweden, was mortally wounded. Charles gave way without a fight, the Scots promising to call a second General Assembly. This re-enacted all the measures taken by the first, and brought a second threat of war. The Scots crossed the Tweed. Charles's army, now under Strafford's command, consisted mainly of conscripts from London, and, ordered to dispute the crossing of the Tyne, they ran away at the first volley of Scottish cannon. The Scots took over the country as far south as York.

Those in England who had been leaders of the opposition to Charles were delighted rather than dismayed by the Scottish victory and demanded that the king should summon a new Parliament. Reluctantly he consented; throughout his reign he had nursed a distrust and dislike of the whole concept of governing with the consent and cooperation of elected representatives. Elections were held amid great excitement, in some places four or five candidates presenting themselves. About two-thirds of the 1640 Parliament were re-elected and John Pym (1584-1643), a west-country MP, already noted for his eloquence, advised his fellow-members to punish those who had planned to alter both the religion and government of the realm by bringing over an army from Ireland. He won general support and Strafford, arrested as he tried to take his seat in the House of Lords, was sent to the Tower of London; a bill of attainder, accusing him of treason, was then brought in. The process was illegal, because he had done nothing outside the powers given him by the king—yet the voting for the bill's third reading was 204 to 59. A mob gathered outside the palace of Whitehall where the king and his family were in residence and howled for Strafford's blood. At the same time William Laud, the aged

Archbishop of Canterbury, who had been as close to the king as Strafford, was impeached by Parliament and sent to the Tower, where he was kept for three years without trial. The English revolution had begun; the royal family was in danger. With a heavy conscience the king signed Strafford's death warrant and he was executed in the presence of a huge crowd on 12 May 1641.

In Parliament attacks on the bishops proceeded in growing heat and anger; those Puritans, said one witness, who hated bishops 'hated them worse than the devil, and they who loved them did not love them so well as they loved their dinner'. Churchmen were shocked to see how in town and country 'cobblers and weavers, feltmongers and tailors, and even butchers, presumed to interpret the word of God'. Clergymen were insulted in the streets and threatened with assault.

In the autumn, moderate opinion was washed away in a tide of fear as news began to come in of a Catholic rebellion in Ireland. At least two thousand Protestants were slain by the insurgents and as many more refugees died of hunger and exposure. In an atmosphere of intense excitement the Puritan leaders in Parliament pushed through the House of Commons what was called a Grand Remonstrance with over a hundred

Warrant in Charles I's own hand for the arrest of five members of the House of Commons and one from the House of Lords on charges of high treason for having taken part in the Grand Remonstrance (1641). It reads:
1. *You are to accuse those Six jointlie and generallie*
2. *You are to reserve the power of making additionalls*
3. *When the Committie for examination is a naming (wch you must press to be close and under tey of secresie) if either Essex, Warwick, Holland, Say, Wharton, or Brooke be names, you must desyre that they may be spared because you ar to examine them as witnesses for me.*

CHARLES R.

(The word on line 4 spelt tey is our word tie, meaning bond)

102

clauses. It set out all their political and religious grievances against the king, and avoided sedition and treason only by the device of saying again and again that it was the king's advisers who had erred and not the king. Oliver Cromwell, a young country member, said that if the Remonstrance had not been passed he would have sold all that he had the next morning and left the country for ever. Charles, urged on by the queen, went to the House of Commons with a large company of armed men and entering the chamber, something no other monarch had done, demanded that the five members principally responsible for the Remonstrance should be handed over to him. They had escaped by a back door and gone down river to take refuge among their friends, the citizens of London. Charles had made plain his opinion that only victory in war could settle the quarrel between him and Parliament.

Open hostilities did not begin at once because Parliament sought compromise not victory. The king raised his standard at Nottingham in 1642. He had only a small force and very little money to pay his men. Parliament, with equally few troops, demanded the surrender of all those who had joined the king. Royalists, feeling this threatened them with the fate of Strafford and Laud, began to send the king money and troops. The opening battles of the civil war went mostly in favour of Charles, but instead of handing over military affairs to experienced soldiers, he imposed his own vacillating command, and failed to press home an attack on London, the source from which Parliament drew financial aid and a large proportion of its foot soldiers.

It was the Scots who ended the stalemate into which by 1643 the war had fallen. Parliament by promising to pay for their military help and to institute 'true religion' (Presbyterianism) in England, an agreement known as the Solemn League and Covenant, achieved its first decisive victory. An army of Scots led by David Leslie, a kinsman of Alexander's, crossed the Tweed early in 1644 and, co-operating with Parliament's New Model army, defeated the Royalists at Marston Moor in July. This might have ended the war, if in Scotland Montrose had not changed sides, and in the king's name looted Aberdeen, conducted a successful clan war against the Campbells in Argyllshire and captured Glasgow.

In England David Leslie refused to be diverted by Montrose. In June 1645 he and the Parliamentary army inflicted final and irreversible defeat on the king at Naseby. Then Leslie, returning to Scotland, overwhelmed Montrose.

Charles had already sent the queen and their elder sons, Charles and James, to the continent for safety. His friend Archbishop Laud had been executed early in 1645. He surrendered to the Scots at Newark in Nottinghamshire in July 1646, and attempted to win by diplomacy what he had lost in war—the right to be an absolute monarch, a course which he pursued with obstinacy and much deceit. On conscientious grounds he refused to do as the Scots wished and abolish Church government by bishops. If he had done so, they would have changed sides and fought for him against his English enemies. Instead they sold him to Parliament in return for a promise of £400,000, part of which they never received.

In 1648 Royalists in Wales, Yorkshire and Essex attempted once more to restore the monarchy by force. This time the Scots were on the king's side, and invaded England by the west coast route. Cromwell's cavalry moved swiftly and unexpectedly across the Pennines and broke up their whole force. Scots taken prisoner were sold to the planters in Barbados at £5 for twenty. The English Royalists still under arms then surrendered, and in dealing with the king the Parliamentary army would hear of no compromise— he had again caused English blood to flow, and he must die. At his trial he refused to admit that the judges appointed by Parliament had any legal status. He was executed in Whitehall on 30 January 1649. Nothing so became him in his life as his courage and dignity in leaving it. Royalist propaganda successfully presented him as a martyr, which he had always meant to be, having refused to save himself either by abdication or flight.

The Commonwealth based its authority on that of the Parliament which had first met eight years before, or rather the Rump of it left after the Army had expelled those members it distrusted. To assert this Parliament's authority in Ireland and Scotland was now of the first importance, since there the Royalists could find plentiful support for a counter-blow. Cromwell was sent to Ireland and in a few weeks had stormed the two east coast towns of Drogheda and Wexford. In his conscientious way he reported in writing to Parliament exactly what happened, how the Irish soldiers were 'decimated' and prisoners again sold for work in Barbados. The English soldiers had in mind the events of 1641, but for what they did in 1649 the Irish did not forgive them.

Six days after Charles I's death the Covenanters in Scotland proclaimed his son Charles King of Great Britain, France and Ireland, and he in return consented to the execution of Montrose, who had done so much for the Royalist cause. The act was typical of that unprincipled determination to regain and keep his throne which marked his whole life. When, in 1650, Cromwell was ordered to end this royalist threat, he marched along the east coast, accompanied by a fleet with supplies. At Dunbar a large force surrounded him, but by a surprise dawn attack on 3 September he put them all to flight, killing, according to his own claim, 3,000 and taking 10,000 prisoners for the

This shows the House of Commons in session presided over by the Speaker in his chair. The legend reads:

IN THE THIRD YEARE OF FREEDOME BY GOD'S BLESSING RESTORED 1651.

An inscription in English instead of Latin was an innovation. It was the third year of the interregnum following the execution of Charles I when the British Isles were ruled by the Rump of the English Parliament elected ten years previously

loss of two officers and twenty men. Scotland, shocked by this disaster, was left a prey to warring parties. The next year Cromwell, hoping to tempt the youthful Charles into an invasion of England, moved north to Perth. The Scots took the bait and marched south by the west coast route, penetrating as far as Worcester. There Cromwell overwhelmed them. Charles's flight from the battle, aided by humble loyalists, was followed by nine years' exile, mainly in Holland. His men were friendless and far from home; not many escaped with their lives.

While Cromwell reigned as Lord Protector (1653-1658), Scotland was better governed than it had been for centuries. Even the Highlands were kept in order, and at Westminster thirty seats were given to Scottish representatives. Yet the whole country resented this loss of independence and looked for a change. When Cromwell died, his son Richard succeeded him, but soon acknowledged himself incapable of governing the country. Of the major generals whom his father had appointed to rule various regions only one proved able to restore order, General Monck, who commanded in Scotland. He marched on London with the intention of holding elections for 'a full and free Parliament'. The Rump was dissolved, and elections began, seats being hotly contested. At the same time Monck sent envoys in secret to Charles II in Holland to suggest terms for his restoration. Charles agreed in the Declaration of Breda to rule in accordance with the wishes of Parliament, and allow freedom of conscience in matters of religious worship.

On 1 May 1660, 'the happiest May Day for many a year', according to the diarist Samuel Pepys, he was welcomed back. This peaceful change, when all had expected another civil war, brought to the majority a feeling of immense relief. Promises made at Breda were not kept; liberty of conscience was not permitted; Quakers and Baptists were persecuted and imprisoned; but such things did not diminish Charles's popularity. He delighted in a system which allowed him to blame the shortcomings of his government on to his ministers; Parliament, he said, was as good as a play, and a mere play it would have become if he had not died at the age of fifty-four. For he had every intention of ruling without Parliament, if need arose. From the moment of his accession James II set about the task of obtaining freedom of worship for his fellow-Catholics, and if he could not do so legally, he planned to use the army. This was at a time when French Huguenots were seeking refuge overseas from the dragoons of Louis XIV's army. Secretly James's opponents invited the ruler of the Dutch Netherlands, William of Orange, to take the throne. On 5 November 1688 he landed with a Dutch army and was crowned king jointly with his wife Mary, the elder of James II's two daughters by his first marriage. Few realised that since William was at war with France England had been committed irretrievably to a long struggle with the richest and most powerful monarchy in Europe. For William the British Isles were but pieces in the deadly game on which the survival of the Dutch republic depended. Yet the Whig Party in England always referred to his invasion as 'the Great and Glorious Revolution'.

The various Acts of Parliament by which William's supporters entrenched the privileges of the Church of England and gave a degree of toleration to some Protestant sects were beneficial in England but disastrous in Ireland. In 1690 a newly elected English Parliament voted William supplies for the reconquest of Ireland, where James II had allowed the Catholics to dispossess Protestants settled there by Cromwell, and drive them behind the walls of Londonderry. There they were saved by English ships when on the point of starvation. William landed in Ulster and, marching on Dublin, was met by James at the crossing of the Boyne. The armies commanded by the two kings were of mixed nationality; there were Irishmen in both camps; James had French officers lent him by Louis XIV; and William had Dutch and Huguenot contingents. When the battle turned against him, James fled with indecent haste to Dublin and on to France. William, to please his English friends, imposed on Ireland a regime of oppression and injustice, flagrantly intolerant in religion. Irish Presbyterians as well as Catholics fled abroad.

In Scotland William was less severe. A Convention of Estates, strongly Presbyterian in composition, abolished episcopacy and repealed all the measures passed under James VII and II for the benefit of Catholics. This did not suit the Highlands and a small force of clansmen under Viscount Dundee defeated the mixed force of Scots and English under General Mackay which met them at Killiecrankie. In the hour of victory, however, Dundee was killed, and the quarrelsome Highlanders, unable to accept another leader, dispersed. The chieftains were required to present themselves and acknowledge William and Mary by the last day of 1691. The chief of the Macdonald clan failed to do so on time and a band of Campbells, who supported William, treacherously offered him hospitality and then murdered him and thirty of his kinsmen at Glencoe. This massacre was remembered when other equally shameful bloodshed was forgotten. For the next fifty years the Highlanders were left to enjoy their own. Though hemmed in by Fort William and a cordon of other strongholds, they proved a ready seed bed for the Jacobite plots of 1715 and 1745.

New Colonies and Trading Posts

One of James I's first acts of foreign policy was to bring the long war with Spain to an end. This was sensible, but unpopular. Both the English and Dutch were trading surreptitiously but profitably with Spanish American ports and peace meant acknowledgement of the Spanish claim to a monopoly of trade between their own colonies and the rest of the world. Royal favour was on the other hand shown to companies and individuals seeking to establish settlements in North America. Between 1607 and 1610 expeditions were sent to Jamestown in Virginia, where the 'planters' prospered because of the discovery that tobacco could be grown for sale in London, where pipe-smoking, a fashion of which King James strongly disapproved, had been made popular by Sir Walter Raleigh. Founding colonies required the investment of large sums lent at great risk. A cash crop like tobacco was therefore especially welcome, affording as it did some quick return for investors. Most colonials, however, lived all their lives without attempting to repay their debts; their creditors were a long way off. In the course of the century Virginia became the wealthiest and most aristocratic of the North American colonies. In the Civil War it welcomed Royalist refugees.

In 1632 another tobacco colony, Maryland, was founded on Chesapeake Bay by Lord Baltimore, a wealthy Irish Catholic, who welcomed co-religionists. Further north,

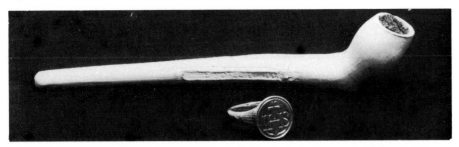

Elizabethan clay pipe (actual size) holding a tiny quantity of tobacco, and finger ring. Pipe-smoking, introduced by Sir Walter Raleigh in 1586, was fashionable only in England. The gold ring, bearing a cross and the sacred monogram IHS, was used as a personal pledge, as in The Merchant of Venice, Act V Scene I. *A similar ring was recently recovered from the underwater wreck of a galley belonging to the Spanish Armada that foundered near the Giant's Causeway in Ireland*

in Massachusetts, a small settlement resulted from the voyage of the *Mayflower* in 1620. About forty of those who sailed in her were Separatists who had fled to Holland from persecution under James I. After thirteen unhappy years there they joined with another forty from England who went in a spirit of adventure.

Their success led to a massive migration of Puritans in 1629 and 1630 led by John Winthrop, a country gentleman from Groton in Suffolk. Later, religious divisions among the people of Massachusetts led to further 'New England' settlements, notably Rhode Island, the work of Anne Hutchinson, for whose colony Roger Williams obtained legal recognition and a constitution allowing religious toleration. During the Civil War New England, though sympathising with Parliament, developed a sense of independence which it never lost, its merchants openly defying laws passed at Westminster to control colonial trade.

Oliver Cromwell, as Lord Protector, reverted to the old anti-Spanish policy, and sent an expedition against the Spanish in the Caribbean which captured Jamaica in 1655. At about the same time the first planting of sugar cane began in Barbados, held since 1624. In the last half of the century the Europeans in the West Indies imported so many negro slaves from Africa that they were soon outnumbered. Some of the islands became entirely dependent on one crop—sugar.

On the Hudson river the early colonies were mainly Dutch, but in 1667 New Amsterdam was taken by the British and renamed New York in honour of Charles II's brother, James, Duke of York. Later in Charles II's reign the king's chronic inability to pay his debts led him to grant a vast stretch of land as personal property to William Penn, the Quaker son of an Admiral who had helped him regain the throne. This became Pennsylvania and to it were attracted Germans, Swedes and Dutch as well as English. Penn, a most original thinker, loved the peace to be enjoyed in America and looking at the wars going on in Europe proposed a Parliament of nations to settle disputes by negotiation.

At the end of the century there was considerable rivalry between those who looked to America for overseas trade and those who argued in favour of India. To develop both trades simultaneously a Scottish financier William Paterson, one of the founders of the Bank of England, proposed a scheme for making a colony at Darien on the Isthmus of Panama. Its object was to dominate trade along both coasts of America and even tranship goods brought across the Pacific from India and the Spice Islands. At first many Englishmen subscribed to the venture, but Darien was Spanish territory and King William, hoping for a Spanish alliance, disapproved. The English withdrew and the Scottish investors, who had raised £350,000, lost all their money. Three expeditions failed in quick succession, the last expelled by the Spaniards. Thousands of would-be settlers died of fever. In Scotland the English were held to be entirely to blame.

On the west coast of Africa Portuguese and Dutch traders had set up a chain of forts. Owing to the general lack of medical knowledge of tropical diseases European settle-

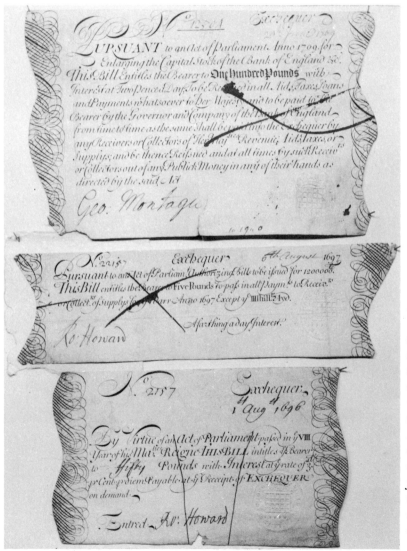

Exchequer Bills of 1696, 1697 and 1709. The 1709 bill, an early form of paper money, entitled the bearer to £100 at interest of 2d. a day 'to be paid by the Governor and Company of the Bank of England'. The Bank was founded in 1694 by leading merchants in the city of London mainly to finance the day-to-day operations of the Government and to obviate the necessity of waiting for tax revenue to be collected

108

Tilbury Fort, built in 1682 on the site of a Tudor fort to guard the north shore of the Thames estuary. The star pattern of its walls incorporated new continental methods of construction seen by Charles II during his exile. Guns placed here and at Gravesend on the south shore would almost certainly have prevented an attack such as the Dutch delivered on the Medway in 1667

ments were impossible, but the first British trading post, that on the Gambia, was acquired in 1686.

In the East Indies there was fierce competition between British and Dutch engaged in the spice trade. In 1623 the Dutch arrested ten Englishmen and some Japanese at Amboina, the centre of the trade. After a trial they were executed. This was always referred to as a 'massacre', and in the successful war which Oliver Cromwell started with the Dutch in 1652 when he was Lord Protector, an indemnity of £88,000 was exacted for the lives lost. The value of the spice trade may be judged by the fact that a single cargo of cloves bought in Amboina for just under £3,000 sold in London for over £36,000. From a Dutch raid on one East Indian island, Pularoon, which the English had planted with nutmeg, a world war resulted, with British and Dutch navies of over 100 ships engaged in the Channel and North Sea (1665-1667).

London before and after Sir Christopher Wren

Ocean trade accelerated the rapid growth of London noticed by many observers in the reign of Elizabeth. The capital could provide the many different services that merchants and seamen needed—a long waterfront with ample wharfage, quiet moorings where ships could be loaded and unloaded from lighters, warehouses for incoming and outgoing cargoes, banks and insurance brokers, middlemen and carriers ready to distribute goods to all parts of Britain by river and road, and in Whitehall, less than three miles away, government officials with invaluable information and advice on foreign affairs.

Both inside and outside the city, details of local government, including the registration of baptisms, marriages and deaths, were a matter for the vestry meetings of the parishes, but within the walls the Lord Mayor and Corporation, an oligarchy of great power and influence, exercised an overall authority. For the crowded poverty-stricken shanty town outside the walls, the various parishes did their best to maintain a semblance of law and order. Before the Great Fire of 1666, which destroyed two-thirds of the city within the walls, the houses of both rich and poor were mainly of wood, and the streets narrow, crowded and dirty. On a hilltop close to the heart of the city the vast half-ruined Gothic cathedral of St Paul rose out of a labyrinth of winding roads and alleys, each with their church towers and graveyards adjoining the foot walks.

In the spring of 1665 reports came in from the parishes outside the walls of deaths attributed to bubonic plague, which had attacked London several times early in the century. The coronation of James I had been postponed a year because of one bad outbreak. As more and more deaths occurred the usual precautions were taken. Medical men at the time suspected that plague infection came from Asia, and ships entering the river with plague cases on board were put in quarantine. It was assumed that plague, like typhus and smallpox, spread by human contact, and so victims were sent to pest houses, and, when these were full, confined to their own houses. This, one pharmacist said at the time, was sheer murder, since the whole household often died of the disease.

The symptoms, a sudden high temperature producing delirium, the formation of nut-like buboes in the groin, hard at first and then suppurating with an evil-smelling pus, black blotches under the skin caused by bursting blood vessels—all these sufferings struck terror, and those whose business did not keep them in town fled to the country. At the peak of the epidemic, which occurred in an exceptionally hot August and September, at least 7,000 died each week over a period of seven weeks. In the cold weather of November, the epidemic ceased, having cost the lives of over 100,000 people.

In September 1666 a fire broke out at night in a baker's shop near the Billingsgate fish market. Fanned by a high wind the fire quickly became uncontrollable. Blowing houses up with gunpowder to cause fire breaks proved useless; the wind veered but did not drop; in four days the heritage of centuries was reduced to ashes, two-thirds of the city within the walls was left a waste. The slums outside were not touched. Even stone buildings perished—St Paul's and eighty-nine other medieval churches suffered irreparable damage.

Within three weeks of this holocaust a young architect, Christopher Wren, educated at Westminster School and Oxford, a fine mathematician with connections at court, had presented plans for re-building. Wren, admiring the Italian renaissance style, and in particular the work of Bernini, had sketched broad straight streets, staircases, porticos and piazzas, all of which the city fathers decided were too expensive.

With the ecclesiastical authorities Wren was more successful. After much argument and several changes of plan his new St Paul's began to rise, reminiscent of St Peter's in Rome, but full of subtle concessions to the clergy who longed to keep the cruciform

Wren's Design for St Paul's. This shows how Wren planned to support the weight of the lantern and cross on a cone of brickwork between the inner and outer skin of the dome. At the time he made this drawing he intended to have the interior of the dome decorated in mosaic depicting scenes from St Paul's life. Eventually this was done by mural painting

plan of the Middle Ages and were pleased with the soft honey-coloured stone brought down from the Cotswolds and the hard stone from Portland. The cost was met by a surcharge on every cauldron of coal brought into the port of London, and out of the mist and smoke of the city rose a building so beautiful that it seemed to float like a mirage above the chimney tops.

The merchants gradually recovered from the loss of their offices, warehouses and homes and of their much loved parish churches, which they began to replace. Wren was the architect everyone wanted. For his ardent spirit no commission was too difficult and none over-taxed his inventiveness and originality. Over fifty churches designed by him adorned the new capital.

In addition to all this ecclesiastical work Wren found time to build a palace for Charles II at Greenwich, a library for Trinity College, Cambridge, the Royal Hospital at Chelsea and a vast new wing at Hampton Court for William III, who considered Kensington Palace bad for his asthma. At Greenwich there was already an Inigo Jones' house, built for Anne of Denmark, James I's queen, but not finished before her death. It had later passed to Henrietta Maria, Charles I's queen. The design must have astonished the court for, unlike Tudor mansions, it had no large dining hall, its rooms being comparatively small and suited to family use. When Wren was asked to plan a palace there he set his own buildings round an open quadrangle leading to the water's edge, and connected by porticos to the queen's house. From the river the background to these two English masterpieces is the steep green slope of the hill on which stands the former Royal Observatory. Of this the oldest part was also built by Wren for Charles II's Astronomer Royal, Flamsteed, who was directed 'to find out the longitude of places, for perfecting navigation and astronomy'. For this laboratory Thomas Tompion constructed what was then the world's most accurate clock, and as a time signal a black globe was lowered from the top of a flagstaff at precisely one o'clock each day and the correct hour, so vital to mariners, sent by semaphore to all important towns.

The new London never again suffered an outbreak of bubonic plague, and the reason for this immunity is mysterious. It is now known that bubonic plague epidemics began with outbreaks among black rats, that is Asiatic house rats which, unlike brown rats, lived in close proximity to human beings. The wooden houses of old London therefore provided ideal homes for them, and plague was spread by *Xenopsylla cheopis*, a type of flea living in their fur as a parasite which multiplied with great rapidity in the hot weather of 1665. The London rats must first have been infected by rats brought by ships from the east. A flea which sucked the blood of a plague-stricken rat became 'blocked' by the plague bacillus breeding in the blood held in its stomach, and, becoming ferociously hungry, attacked human beings. It was, however, unable, having punctured the human skin, to take in blood, and injected the plague-bearing blood. Theoretically plague victims could have been safely nursed by their families, provided that they and their surroundings were kept clear of fleas. Flight from plague, though at the time universally considered liable to spread the disease, in fact greatly reduced its danger.

Science under Royal Patronage

The advance of science was often interrupted and impeded by wars and revolutions but in no previous century did the ideas of scientists on what was then called natural philosophy change more quickly or more fundamentally. In medicine the great discoveries of the sixteenth century had been mainly in anatomy, but physiology was unable to progress without a correct explanation of how blood circulated. This was supplied in 1628 by William Harvey (1578-1657), who had studied at Cambridge and Padua, and had made long series of experiments on living animals. He calculated that a human heart must take about half an hour to pump all the blood in the body through the arteries and receive it back through the veins, and the total quantity of blood amounted to about six litres. In the Civil War he took no part in politics, but was deprived by Parliament of his living at London's oldest hospital, St Bartholomew's, because Charles I had taken a great interest in his work and supplied him with animals for it. He tutored Charles's sons, and probably gave Charles II his life-long interest in scientific affairs.

In the last years of the Commonwealth a group of Oxford men devoted to science formed the nucleus of the Royal Society founded under Charles II. Among its leaders were Christopher Wren and Robert Boyle (1627-1691), the seventh son and fourteenth child of the Earl of Cork. Boyle lifted chemistry out of the trammels of alchemy by demonstrating that the volume of gases varied in precisely inverse proportion to the pressure upon them. Cambridge was equally productive of men of genius, the most influential being Isaac Newton (1642-1727). His work on the theory of gravitation was published in 1686 through the encouragement of the astronomer Edmund Halley, who, from observing the brilliant comet that appeared in 1682, was able to predict correctly its next appearance in 1759.

Newton's gifts were so many-sided that he was appointed Master of the Royal Mint, then housed in the Tower of London, and helped those who founded the Bank of England in 1694 to carry through a complete re-coinage. A friend remembers him saying towards the end of his life: '*I do not know what I may appear to the world, but to myself I seem to have been only like a boy playing on the seashore and diverting myself in now and then finding a smoother pebble or a prettier shell than ordinary, whilst the great ocean of truth lay all undiscovered before me.*'

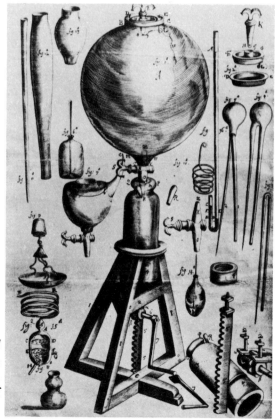

Boyle's air pump, the first constructed in England, used in his experiments on the properties of gases. An illustration from his book Spring and Weight of Air *published in Oxford, 1661*

113

CHAPTER TEN

The Eighteenth Century

The Monarchy

William III	1689–1702
Anne	1702–1714
George I	1714–1727
George II	1727–1760
George III	1760–1820

Wars with France

By 1700 there were few monarchs in either Europe or Asia who did not envy Louis XIV the court of Versailles with its magnificent buildings, gardens and hunting grounds, its throne room, offices of state and circle of philosophers, writers and dramatists. France was the richest and, with the exception of the Russia of Peter the Great, most extensive and populous state in Europe. Her army was the best organised and equipped in the world and officered by men of noble birth proud of the long military tradition of their families.

Already Louis XIV's ambition to extend his kingdom to its 'natural frontier', the Rhine, was half accomplished, and in 1700 it looked as though another of his dreams, 'to abolish the Pyrenees', might also be achieved. Charles II of Spain, dying childless, had left a will naming Louis' grandson Philip V of Spain. If this boy were also to succeed his grandfather in France, not only the Spanish Netherlands (the territory now called Belgium), but the Spanish colonies in North, Central and South America would be joined with France under one ruler. This prospect so tempted Louis XIV that, in violation of his treaty obligations to William III, he accepted on his grandson's behalf, knowing that he would have to fight the supporters of Charles, son of the Austrian Emperor, who was also a claimant for the Spanish crown. Louis was now an ageing and arrogant man, drugged by years of flattery, who was unable to see the consequences of his policies or to respond to contrary advice from friends however loyal.

In England a war to prevent the union of Spain and France was not unwelcome to those with investments in overseas trade, who feared competition from Europe, but it seemed senseless to the landed gentry. These two bitterly opposed factions were, however, united by another act of folly on Louis XIV's part. He promised the dying ex-king James II of England that he would recognise his son James Edward as James III and rightful claimant (Le Prétendant) to the crown of Great Britain and Ireland. For propaganda purposes his enemies in Britain mistranslated this French title; James Edward became known as the Old Pretender and his son, Charles Edward, as the Young Pretender, and the great majority both in England and Scotland, faced with the possibility of a Catholic king being imposed on Britain by a foreign power, forgot their other political differences and rallied round Queen Anne, who declared that she knew in her heart that she was English.

In Europe Britain had as allies against the French and Spanish an imposing list of powers—the Dutch Netherlands, the Holy Roman Empire, the Electorates of Branden-burg, Hanover and the Rhine Palatinate, Denmark, Portugal and Savoy. In practice these friends were often liabilities: they were ill-organised financially and could not fight without British subsidies; and their war aims were limited. To invade France was beyond their powers; to prevent her extending her frontiers was the most that the majority of the allies dared hope to do; to destroy her armies required skill, persistence and great daring, and this the English were to display to an unprecedented degree under John Churchill, Duke of Marlborough, a general whose high intelligence, handsome presence and exquisite manners made him the ideal leader for a force of mixed nationality. In 1704, after careful preparations in Holland, he set out with an allied army for a secret destination, determined to save the Austrian Empire from the French by stopping their advance along the upper Danube valley. When news came that he had left the Rhine and was crossing the Black Forest opponents of the government in Parliament were furious. The allied artillery alone required 2,000 horses to drag the guns over the hilly roads. Defeat would have meant a rout, but at Blenheim on 13 August 1604 Marlborough won a great but costly victory. Nearly a quarter of his force of 52,000 were killed or wounded. Of the 9,000-strong British contingent over 2,000 were lost. The French on the other hand had been so completely out-generalled that whole regi-ments surrendered, and their losses, including those during the retreat, amounted to 40,000.

The fruits of this victory were wasted. The fighting dragged on, in spite of Marlborough's further victories in Flanders—Ramillies in 1706, Oudenarde in 1708 and Malplaquet in 1709. By the peace of Utrecht in 1713 it was agreed that the crowns of France and Spain should not be united; that the British should retain Gibraltar, captured in 1704, and the French colony now known as Nova Scotia; and that the Austrians should rule the former Spanish Netherlands.

During the war British and Dutch overseas trade had been severely harassed. Merchant ships, forced to travel in convoy with naval escorts, had not always evaded capture by French privateers operating out of Breton ports and from Dunkirk, where gun-carrying galleys were kept. These bombarded English ports and attacked shipping in calm weather when they could not be chased. The oarsmen were Huguenots and Turkish prisoners of war, who were released when the British captured the port, dismantled the fortifications and filled in the harbour.

For some time after the settlement at Utrecht there was no major European war, but the emergence of a new and aggressive state, the kingdom of Prussia, once more upset the balance of power. The Prussians, an industrious Protestant people of mixed race, accustomed from medieval times to the harsh, military rule of the Teutonic Knights, had created under a succession of eccentric but able rulers a fine army and an efficient civil service. During the reign of Frederick the Great they used this power without scruple, breaking obligations to Austria and annexing Silesia, part of the hereditary domain of the first empress, Maria Theresa. Later, the discovery that the soil of Silesia was rich in minerals was to add immensely to the military might of the Prussian state.

In 1756 the French and Austrians allied themselves with the Empress of Russia to attack Frederick the Great and force him to return the stolen province. The British, being involved in German affairs because George II was Elector of Hanover, sent an army to fight on the Prussian side and won an important victory over a French army at Minden in central Germany in 1759. Prussia, surrounded by enemies, was enabled to survive partly through Frederick's military skill, partly by British aid.

The war that began in Europe in 1756 and lasted seven years broke out earlier between the British and French colonies in North America, where the French were attempting to link their settlements in Canada with those on the Mississippi. Such a link would have blocked the westward thrust of American frontiersmen. The danger ended when, under the leadership of William Pitt, later created Earl of Chatham, the British army, acting in close concert with the navy, sailed six hundred miles up the St Lawrence valley and under General James Wolfe captured Quebec in 1759.

When peace was concluded at Paris in 1763 the French settlers were allowed to stay on the St Lawrence under British rule but those in Louisiana remained free. The British on both sides of the Atlantic were well aware that they had won an empire, the French unaware that they had lost one. Only fifteen years later they took their revenge by rousing up most of Europe against the British when a revolution began in the American colonies. Co-operation between the British army and navy was as faulty in this war as it had been efficient in 1759. The navy was distracted by the need to fight the French and Spaniards on both sides of the Atlantic, and to face the Armed Neutrality of Russia, Prussia, Sweden and Denmark. When peace was made in Paris in 1783, the British were forced to recognise the United States of America, a federal republic to which belonged thirteen former British colonies with a total population of over 3,000,000.

The French monarchy paid dearly for aiding American rebels imbued with republican ideals. Not only had the war added enormously to the French government's crushing debts but the egalitarian traditions of America, represented in Paris by the outstanding personality of Benjamin Franklin during the war, had encouraged revolutionary ideas among the idle rich. Louis XVI, a man whose passion in life was hunting, could not conceive that the absolute monarchy he had inherited could be in danger. Even after the capture of the Bastille by the Paris mob on 14 July 1789, the able young Prime Minister of England, William Pitt, predicted a period of European peace. Within three years Europe was plunged into the first of a series of wars that lasted for twenty-two years. In August 1792 the Jacobin revolutionary Danton organised a Paris mob which murdered the king's Swiss guard, captured the Tuileries Palace, and imprisoned the royal family.

Seals of our Arms to be affixed thereto.

*Done at Paris this third Day of Sept.
the Year of our Lord, one thousand seven hundred
hty three.*

D Hartley

John Adams

Franklin

John Jay

Treaty of Paris, 3 September 1783. This treaty marked the end of the American War of Independence. It was signed on behalf of the United States of America by John Adams, Benjamin Franklin and John Jay and by David Hartley MP on behalf of Great Britain. John Jay was elected President of the Continental Congress, 1778. John Adams was second President of the USA

By then even the prudent emperor, Leopold of Austria, had been persuaded to invade France and give aid to his sister Queen Marie Antoinette and her husband. Instead his intervention hastened their death by the guillotine. The presence of foreign soldiers on French soil, by giving the revolutionaries the aura of patriotism, stimulated the recruitment of an all-but invincible army. The ghost of Louis XIV haunted once more the headquarters of the French generals; the Rhine must indeed be 'the natural frontier of France', and the Austrian and Dutch Netherlands, already thoroughly infiltrated by the partisans of the new regime, must be brought at last under one government. The revolutionary ardour of the French and the military incompetence of their enemies soon made these ambitions a reality and the results of the battle of Blenheim were reversed. Britain entered the nineteenth century without an effective ally anywhere in Europe, and with her ancient enemy mistress of the entire coastline from the borders of Denmark to the Pyrenees.

The Jacobites and the Union of the English and Scottish Parliaments
William III, who died in 1702 after a riding accident, gave his consent on his deathbed

to an Act of Succession. It was already obvious that though Anne had borne many children, none was likely to survive her, and so it was arranged that the crown should go to George, the middle-aged Protestant Elector of Hanover, a greatgrandson of James I. The opposition to the Hanoverian succession was strongest in the Gaelic-speaking central and western Highlands of Scotland, but even in London and within court circles there were secret communications with James Edward and his son. It is now clear that after the 1688 Revolution a Stuart restoration was never a practical possibility, but at the time Jacobites, because they lived in an atmosphere of conspiracy, imagined that the Pretenders had a host of friends. Most Scots, however, knew that no Stuart would have tolerated the freedom of speech and independence of character shown in the Scottish parliaments of William III, and under Queen Anne there seemed at first little hope of a union of parliaments which the English, faced with a long war against France, considered essential for the safety of the island. Yet the Scots behaved as if they were benefactors rather than beneficiaries and insisted they should be allowed all the privileges of the English in foreign trade without offering anything in return.

The arguments about union in the Scottish Parliament were long and scholarly, the differences of opinion deep and sincere. The possibility of setting up an independent

Two pamphlets typify the deep division of Scottish opinion on Parliamentary Union

republic was among the solutions discussed, for the Dutch constitution was much admired. Under it William III had been succeeded by an official called the Grand Pensionary, but in the end a Treaty of Union was drawn up, debated and signed, together with statutes recognising the Presbyterian structure of the Church of Scotland, the Scottish system of education and the continuation of the Scottish courts of law with their Romano-Dutch concepts. These examples of forbearance by a strong power in dealing with a small and weak neighbour bore fruit. The union of 1707 proved enduring in spite of two Jacobite rebellions and numerous Scottish complaints. Forty-five members represented Scotland in the House of Commons and sixteen peers in the House of Lords. Scots were accepted and won fame as ministers of the Crown, and as soldiers and sailors. In law and medicine Scots soon occupied leading positions.

The Pretender, James Edward, realised that, if Union succeeded, his chances of recovering the throne would diminish still further. In 1708 he persuaded Louis XIV to assign him a naval and military force for a descent on the east coast of Scotland, where, it was hoped, the Jacobites would answer a call to arms. Storms, and quarrels among the French commanders, delayed the expedition, and James, finding no great support, returned without landing. The British government arrested some leading Jacobites, and one, the aged Lord Griffin, died a prisoner in the Tower.

This failure deprived the Pretender of most of his support in France, but in 1715 the Regent of France (Louis XIV had died earlier in the year) promised help if the Jacobites could first show their strength. The Earl of Mar, who had earlier supported Union, changed sides and 'raised the clans', that is, ordered tenants of military age to follow their lords to war. War, however, was different from the organised raiding and looting for which the clansmen were fitted. Faced with disciplined troops armed with muskets and bayonets, and supported by field artillery and cavalry, they were expected to charge on foot armed chiefly with claymores, daggers and small shields. None the less 12,000 men joined Mar—Camerons, Drummonds, Gordons, Macdonalds, Macleans, Mackenzies, Macphersons, Macintoshes, Macgregors, Murrays, Ogilvies and Robertsons. There were old scores to settle; the Macdonalds and Macleans yearned to meet the Campbells. In the north the pro-government clans, Frasers, Mackays, Munroes, Rosses and Sutherlands, retained control. The Jacobite clans soon took Perth, and sent a force south into Lancashire as far as Preston. In November Mar, having fought an indecisive action against government troops led by the Duke of Argyll at Sheriffmuir, retreated, and the force in Lancashire was compelled to surrender. Too late the Pretender arrived; in despair he ordered the clansmen to save themselves by dispersing. Among the prisoners taken at Preston Lords Kenmure, Derwentwater and Nithsdale were condemned to death, but Nithsdale escaped from the Tower. Shiploads of humbler Scots were sent to the West Indian plantations as slave labour.

Ten years later Sir Robert Walpole's government adopted wiser policies for the Highlands. General Wade was appointed to command there and he drove 260 miles of good military roads with fine stone bridges up into the hills to link Perth with Inverness and the Great Glen. He also recruited soldiers among the clansmen, forming the Black Watch, the 42nd regiment of foot.

Glenfinnan, Invernesshire. Here, in June 1745, about 1,200 Highlanders assembled in answer to Prince Charles Edward's call to armed rebellion in support of the Jacobite cause

Scotland was not grateful for these benefits and the taxes which the government imposed on malt and salt were so unpopular that riots resulted. Smugglers became public heroes, and when one was caught and condemned to death, the crowd at the place of execution threatened to rescue him. The soldiers present were ordered by their commander, Captain Porteous, to fire. They did so, killing several people. For this a Scottish court condemned Porteous to death. He was reprieved but still in prison when a mob broke in and lynched him. For this crime the Edinburgh authorities could find no suspects, and so Queen Caroline, deputising for her husband George II, who was in Germany, proposed to arrest the Provost and punish the city. This was thought unreasonable, and she had to be content with exacting a fine of £2,000 to be paid to Porteous's widow.

In 1745 the son of the Pretender, Charles Edward, whose mother was a Polish princess living in Rome, was twenty-five. His education had been neglected, but he was handsome and brave. Having set out from France with seven supporters and having

120

landed in the Outer Isles, he raised his standard at Glenfinnan on 19 August—too late in the year. Owing to the military blunders of the government he captured Edinburgh a month later, and, beating a small English force at Prestonpans, set out for London with only 5,000 clansmen and 300 cavalry, taking the west coast route and reaching Derby in December. There he turned back, and, far to the north, at Culloden Moor near Inverness, the remnant of his forces was overwhelmed by a strong army under the Duke of Cumberland, well-named 'Butcher', for on his orders the wounded were dispatched where they lay, the fugitives hunted down and slain, their crofts burnt, and their families evicted. Three Jacobite lords were publicly executed in London. This time the Highlanders were deprived of all their arms. The pro-government clans suffered with the rest under the Proscription Act, which also forbade the making or wearing of clan tartans. For five months Prince Charles remained in hiding in the hills, his protectors known, but never betrayed. At last he escaped in a French frigate. There was sorrow in all the glens; in some, silence.

Farmers and Improvers

Just as the dynastic wars of the eighteenth century sprang from the medieval habit of regarding kingdoms and empires as the personal property of those who inherited titles to them, so in many counties medieval customs still governed the countryman's life. Over large tracts of the midlands and south the open-field system of communal agriculture persisted. One of its chief drawbacks was that a third of the land was left fallow every year. Farmers were unable to keep more than a few beasts through the winter and so had insufficient manure to replenish the soil; fallowing was the only way to avoid exhausting it. In addition a lazy minority, by letting weeds grow on their land, not working on sunny days, neglecting livestock in bad weather and other failings could cause a whole community to suffer. 'Improvers' found a number of ways out of these difficulties; by exchange, purchase or Act of Parliament the holdings, instead of being left in strips scattered over the open fields, often 500 acres in extent, were concentrated, and enclosed within quickset hedges or drystone walls, the new fields varying in size and shape according to the nature of the soil, but being generally about ten acres each. The uncultivated 'waste' lying between one village and another was also divided up and enclosed, having first been stripped of trees, bracken and heather, except where these were needed as coverts for fox and pheasant. Lastly, the common rights of the villages in matters of grazing were bought out and the commons apportioned between those willing to cultivate them. The new beauty of hedgerow, copse and wall replaced the old, wild, unkempt loveliness. Something of the old England was, however, preserved by landowners like Henry Hoare at Stourhead in Wiltshire, who pioneered the change from the stiff formality of French gardens to the naturalness of a 'landscape' garden. Round the new Palladian mansions 'Capability' Brown also laid out miniature hills, lakes and woods which were a welcome contrast to the cold severity of classical architecture.

The pressure of the French wars, which raised the price of corn, accelerated these changes and, though they brought misery and injustice to some, they enormously

(*above*) *Chiswick House, Middlesex. This villa, completed in 1736 by Lord Burlington and built for himself in conjunction with the architect William Kent, was modelled on the Italian architect Palladio's Villa Capra near Vincenza, which Burlington had seen. The style became highly fashionable throughout Britain, though seldom used with such fine taste as here. The planting of cedars of Lebanon near such houses also became a favourite practice. Only the descendants of the planters could hope to enjoy the shade of such magnificent but slow-growing trees;*
(*left*) *Chiswick House Portico*

Saxtead Green Post Mill, Suffolk. Mills of this type were once common, being used to grind wheat. The whole of the white wooden superstructure could be turned on a central post by one man to face the prevailing wind. Great skill was needed to judge the weather and prevent the heavy arms from revolving in winds of gale force

increased the wealth of the country as a whole. Many farmers travelled from county to county studying the work of the most intelligent and successful landowners, among whom Lord Townshend (1674-1738), Robert Bakewell (1723-1795), and Thomas Coke (1752-1842), who was raised to the peerage as Earl of Leicester, were especially admired.

Lord Townshend, a brother-in-law of Sir Robert Walpole, and a gifted statesman, lived in retirement during the last eight years of his life on his estates at Raynham in Norfolk. Finding much of his land little better than rabbit pasture he made it fertile by a four-course rotation of root and grain, which rendered the old fallowing unnecessary and provided supplies of turnips for winter stock feed. This seemed too revolutionary to other farmers at first but later his ideas were adopted with success.

Robert Bakewell, who inherited a 440-acre farm at Dishley, Leicestershire, in 1760, became England's first scientific stockbreeder, producing sheep that were ready for slaughter in two years. Thomas Coke, who was also keenly interested in stockbreeding, had estates at Holkham in Norfolk, where he gave his tenant farmers the security of long leases but wrote into them terms requiring new methods. His slogan was: 'No fodder, no beasts; no beasts, no manure; no manure, no crop.' The price of such leases rose steeply, so that his estate, which in 1776 yielded only £12,332, was worth £25,789 by 1816. Sheep-shearing at Holkham and on the Duke of Bedford's estate at Woburn in

AND HE GAVE IT FOR HIS OPINION

that whoever could make two ears of corn or two blades of grass to grow upon a spot of ground where only one grew before would deserve better of mankind and do more essential service to his country than the whole race of politicians put together.

From "A Voyage to Brobingnag," the second part of "Gulliver's Travels," by Jonathan Swift. D.W.S. Benney, scripsit

Johnathan Swift (1667-1745) was a satirist whose command of English made him greatly feared in his lifetime, yet Gulliver's Travels *became a favourite children's book*

Bedfordshire became great annual festivals at which hundreds of guests, including foreign visitors, were lavishly entertained.

The effect of the new supplies of meat on the standard of living in the towns may be judged from one of many cases investigated at the time by Sir Frederic Eden in a survey of the conditions of the poor. In 1795 a Leicester woolcomber, whose family of four lived on his earnings and those of his wife and elder son, plus £11 from the Poor Law, amounting to £47 a year in all, were in the habit of buying weekly 10 lb of butcher's meat, 2 lb of butter, $3\frac{1}{2}$ lb of cheese and about 19 pints of milk as well as potatoes, vegetables, tea, sugar and beer.

Both the king, in his capacity as a great landlord, and the government played a part in making British agriculture the most advanced in the world. George III took great pride in his nickname of Farmer George and was devoted to his model farm at Windsor. He also made a personal friend of Arthur Young, the foremost writer on agricultural affairs, who travelled ceaselessly inspecting farms where new methods were being tried. Young was made Secretary to the Board of Agriculture, a semi-official body founded in 1793 whose first President, Sir John Sinclair of Caithness (1754-1835), not only was a successful exponent of new methods on his own estates, but organised a remarkable series of statistical surveys informing the government on the size of farms, average rentals and other matters. In the twenty years following the foundation of the Board 1,883 Enclosure Acts were passed through Parliament bringing into cultivation 2,260,000 acres, but the Board was constantly pointing to the 22,000,000 acres uncultivated, though capable of yielding crops. One speaker mentioned in Sir John's Memoirs said: 'Let us not be satisfied with the liberation of Egypt [from Napoleon] or the subjugation of Malta, but let us subdue Finchley Common: let us conquer Hounslow Heath, let us compel Epping Forest to submit to the yoke of improvement.'

Fire Engines and Oxygen

The first application of steam power to industry was achieved early in the century through an invention by Thomas Newcomen (1663-1729) of Dartmouth. This fire-

124

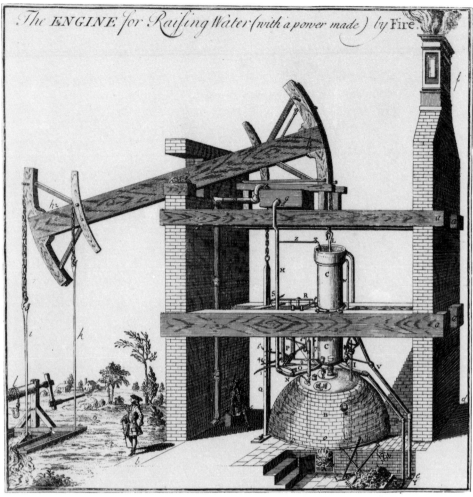

A 1717 engraving of Newcomen's 'fire' engine engaged on pumping water from a mine

engine, as it was called, was stationary and worked at atmospheric pressure. The up-and-down motion of its horizontal beam made it suitable for pumping out water from mines and similar work, but not for driving machinery needing rotary action. Hitherto most coalmine shafts had been driven up into the sides of hills so that water entering them could drain off by gravity. With steam pumps shafts could be sunk below pit end level.

Another use for Newcomen engines was found at Abraham Darby's iron works at Coalbrookdale in Shropshire. About 1710 Darby constructed a furnace with water-driven bellows and so obtained a coke from the local coal with which iron could be smelted in unprecedented quantities. The Newcomen engine was employed for pumping up a good head of water above the wheel driving the bellows. His son and grandson, Abraham Darby II and III, introduced further improvements and their example was followed on other iron fields. By the end of the century most iron works smelted with coke, and skilled craftsmen from Sussex, where for centuries iron works had used charcoal

Watt's rotative beam engine 1788

made in the forest of the Weald, moved northwards, some being attracted to the Carron works in Scotland.

It was James Watt (1734-1819) who devised a radical change in Newcomen's fire-engine. At the age of twenty-one he was an instrument maker working at Glasgow University for Professor Black, who asked him to repair a Newcomen engine used by his students. In effect Watt made a new engine with a special condensing chamber separate from the cylinder and a piston that operated entirely by direct steam pressure, and in 1769, after five years of trial and error, perfected his first engine and went into business. He obtained his metal from the Darbys; his cylinders from John Wilkinson, the sword-maker; and financial backing from Matthew Boulton of Birmingham. Between 1775 and 1800 Boulton and Watt erected steam engines at 84 cotton mills, 30 collieries, 28 iron works, 22 copper mines, 18 canals and 17 breweries besides a number of engines for overseas customers.

Watt also helped to revolutionise the methods of bleaching cotton and linen fabrics, which had previously been processed with sour milk and exposure to air, sometimes taking eight months. After a visit to France in 1786, he brought back details of

126

Berthollet's method using chlorine, and this was tried out in Glasgow with great success, reducing the time to a few days.

A more fundamental discovery in chemistry was taken from England to France. Joseph Priestley, a Nonconformist minister famous for his unorthodox theology, studied chemistry as a pastime, like many learned men of the day. When using a burning glass on red calx of mercury he obtained metallic mercury and a gas with extraordinary properties. No explanation could be given for this, as it was contrary to all current theories on combustion until, in 1774, on a visit to Paris he met Antoine Lavoisier, a young chemist already famous. Priestley described his experiment and Lavoisier, intensely interested, started further experiments on the same lines. He succeeded in proving that air was composed of two gases, oxygen (the name was his invention) and nitrogen, and that oxygen was a component of most acids. Unfortunately, revolutionaries brought his career to an untimely end, sending him to the guillotine in 1794.

Communications by Road and Water

The enclosure of the open fields and commons sometimes had an adverse effect on highways by confining them to two carriageways and spoiling their drainage. Under the careless old system it was not considered objectionable for a vehicle coming to a muddy patch or hole to swing out into the adjoining common and follow a parallel but drier course. The 'right of passage' legally entitled drivers to do so; they were not guilty of trespass. In certain counties, such as Kent and Sussex, where fields had been generally enclosed in medieval times, the roads were notoriously bad because the hedges forced vehicles to pass and re-pass on the same tracks, which naturally became deeply rutted.

The upkeep of roads was the responsibility of parishes, but its cost led to much inefficiency and neglect. In 1706 Parliament therefore created the first Turnpike Trust, giving it powers to erect toll-gates and to charge all road-users specified rates. In 1716 parishes were permitted to pay turnpike trusts the equivalent of what they had formerly spent on the upkeep of roads. Not all did so, and for a long time the main highways consisted of stretches still under parishes and others, much improved, under turnpike trusts. In 1735 and 1750 there were serious riots in which toll-gates and toll-houses were destroyed. This violence grew out of a dislike of 'London' government; people objected to paying tolls for what had previously been 'free'; the idea that the new roads would add to the general wealth of the community had little appeal.

The turnpike trusts were nonetheless a success and employed men of a new profession, road engineers, among whom John Metcalfe (1717-1810), 'Blind Jack of Knaresborough', Thomas Telford (1757-1834), a Scottish shepherd's son, and John McAdam (1756-1836), an Ayrshire landowner, were the foremost. Metcalfe, working in Yorkshire, showed the importance of firm foundations, a cambered surface and drains at the road sides to carry off storm water. McAdam became the leading turnpike engineer in the west of England and also in the London area, where he brought order out of chaos. Telford, a noted builder of bridges and aqueducts, did not engineer his greatest roads until after 1800, when he built the new London-Holyhead route for the Irish mail coaches and revolutionised communications by road and water in the Highlands of Scotland. He insisted on deep foundations and gentle gradients which made his roads much more expensive than those of McAdam, who was satisfied as long as his methods produced hard well-rolled surfaces that threw water off.

The design of coaches and waggons in the first half of the century did not permit high speeds, for which steel springs were necessary, but when these became available the demand for better roads was universal. Coaches belonging to one company would race against those of another, not always to the benefit of passengers. Accidents on corners were frequent, since differential gears had not been invented. Nevertheless, speeds increased and between 1750 and 1800 the average time for a journey from London to Edinburgh was reduced from twelve to four days; and that from London to Newcastle-on-Tyne took from six days in 1750 to three in 1775.

Coaches relied on inns to supply them with fresh horses for each stage and to do running repairs. There were grooms, ostlers, saddlers, and blacksmiths ready to change teams and see harness and shoes were in order. Stabling was also provided, sometimes for as many as two hundred horses. As soon as a coach drew off the road into an inn yard, the tired horses were taken out of the shafts, the coach turned round and the new team put in harness.

In 1784 John Palmer of Reading secured a contract from the government for carrying mails in fast coaches with new patent springs. Previously mails had been delivered by postboys on horseback. Letters at this time were either franked by a Member of Parliament or paid for by the addressee. Poor people sometimes sent letters on which relatives unable to pay the postal charge could see their handwriting and know they were well, before refusing to accept delivery.

Mail coaches increased facilities available for the well-to-do, taking four passengers inside but none outside. Slower, bigger coaches provided cheaper seats outside, though for long journeys most fares were beyond the pockets of artisans. Workmen attracted by news of good wages in distant towns travelled on foot, wearing the clothes and caps of their trade and lodging on the way at trade clubs. Occasionally they would pay to ride on stage-waggons conveying goods from town to town or get lifts from local carriers.

Owing to the high cost of horse-drawn transport, the numerous slow-flowing rivers of England had been the main means of transport for heavy goods. A horse working along a towpath could pull thirty times the weight he could draw on a road. If the depth of water was insufficient, or too variable for laden boats, barriers were built with movable sections in mid-stream. For downstream traffic the middle section was opened to let through a 'flash' of water carrying the boats with it. Horses and hauliers could sometimes also drag boats upstream at such places. All through the eighteenth century river 'navigations' were being improved by private companies.

The Irwell navigation near Manchester was used by the young Duke of Bridgewater for carrying coal from his mines at Worsley but it was costly and unreliable. He therefore asked James Brindley, a millwright, to design a canal to take the coal. Brindley, a self-taught Derbyshire man, decided to build a seven-mile waterway and carry it over the river Irwell on an aqueduct at Barton. Though this had cost the duke £200,000 by opening day in 1761, it was a great financial success. Soon he extended it for twenty-four miles to a point on the Mersey tideway fifteen miles above Liverpool.

Brindley's name had been given to the duke by Lord Gower, who had asked him to plan a canal linking the Mersey and the Trent, and this was now begun. A canal-building fever followed, Brindley himself designing 360 miles of waterway. He was against locks, considering them time-wasting and costly and choosing longer routes at continuous levels wherever possible. His successors were more ambitious and many lock stairs were constructed. By 1794 a great 'cross' of main canals with numerous feeders linked the Mersey, Humber, Thames and Severn. This network with Birmingham at its centre became as important to the early stages of the Industrial Revolution as railways were in the latter.

Religion and Education

The removal of some of the legal disabilities under which nonconformists had suffered in Charles II's reign enabled them to start a number of schools where pupils paid such fees as they could afford and were supported by voluntary contributions. These efforts were emulated by an Anglican body, founded in 1698 and called the Society for the Propagation of Christian Knowledge, which had, by the end of Queen Anne's reign, provided schools for 5,000 boys and girls in the London area and probably 20,000 more scattered among other major towns. They did not depend on the support of a few wealthy founders. In the parish of St Margaret's, Westminster, for example, a cheese-monger, a draper, a bookseller and three general dealers in soap, candles, brooms and leather goods called a meeting to consider the state of the parish and 'did think it proper and convenient to erect a free school where forty of the greatest objects of charity should be educated in sober and virtuous principles and instructed in the Christian religion'. The tradesmen met every week to supervise the school; provided grey coats for the children and grey yarn for their parents to knit stockings; and persuaded their own wives to make the children caps and bands. They also instructed the schoolmaster 'to win the love and affection of the children and thereby encourage them, rather than by correction force them, to learn'. When the pupils were old enough they were carefully placed with good employers as apprentices in various trades and crafts.

In spite of a number of scandals inevitable in a system organised by people of moderate means and therefore excessively concerned with keeping down costs, the charity schools prospered throughout the century, and one of their annual gatherings in St Paul's was described in glowing terms by the poet William Blake (1757-1827) in one of his 'Songs of Innocence'. He had a keen eye for hypocrisy and often castigated the cruelties he observed around him, yet his testimony to the spirit of the age is in sharp contrast to the often-quoted remark made by the French philosopher Montesquieu after a visit in the 1720s: 'There is no religion in England. If anyone mentions religion, people begin to laugh.'

Among the laymen who took their Christian responsibilities seriously was a retired sea captain, Thomas Coram (1668-1751), who succeeded, after pleading for seventeen years, in obtaining a royal charter for a Foundling Hospital in London. Babies, frequently to be found abandoned in the streets, were taken in, nursed and later trained in useful crafts. The chief objection to Coram's scheme was that it would encourage immorality. Fortunately he had the support of several outstanding people—the composer Handel (1685-1759) gave the Hospital an organ; the painter Hogarth (1697-1764) a picture of Moses in the bulrushes and a brilliant portrait of the founder.

One of those who assisted Coram, General Oglethorpe, also went to the rescue of those in prison for not paying their debts, and organised the American colony of Georgia as a place where they might be sent to make a fresh start. The colony attracted a young Oxford don, John Wesley (1703-1791), a Church of England clergyman, uncertain of his vocation. Other students, noting his habits of hard work and churchgoing, had sneeringly called him a Methodist. His stay in Georgia was not successful, but through it he met some Moravians whose form of Protestant belief and practice appealed to him strongly. Soon after his return he began a life of missionary work among the poor and outcast whom the Church of England, with its cumbersome parish organisation, had failed to reach—among them tin miners in Cornwall and coalminers in Wales and the north. The unorthodox enthusiasm of his followers encountered not only the jealous hostility of the leaders of the Church and the upper classes, but the sticks and stones of ignorant

John Wesley (1703-1791). A statue standing on land he bought for his followers in Bristol. The founder of Methodism, he travelled on horseback for many years riding night and day on lonely unlit roads

mobs. He was at first reluctant to preach out of doors, but from 1740 travelled ceaselessly for fifty years, giving fifteen sermons a week, and covering 5,000 miles a year. Wesley died a clergyman of the Church of England, but he had in effect set up a church within a church, and after his death his converts, about 60,000 in all, reacted sharply against Anglicanism, setting up their own chapels with ministers serving them in rotation. Later the Methodists split into different sects, determined largely by their views on business and politics. All the sects, however, encouraged men and women in habits of self-education and strenuously opposed such social evils as the drink trade and slavery.

The Anti-Slavery Movement

In the latter half of the eighteenth century a small association of men under the influence of Quakerism, Methodism and the Evangelical movement in the Church of England completely reversed public opinion on slavery and the negro slave trade, which had previously been accepted as part of the natural order. The slaves were bought from West African chieftains and taken across the Atlantic for sale to planters growing sugar in the West Indies, coffee in Brazil and tobacco and cotton in the southern colonies of North America. About half the shipping engaged was British and the rest came from France, the Netherlands and other countries in western Europe. The ramifications of the trade affected almost every branch of the national economy; there were the manufacturers who provided the goods that others used as barter for slaves in Africa and merchants who imported molasses and rum from the Caribbean, for the slave ships did a triangular run, outward bound to West Africa, then westwards to America, and lastly home. So many interests, so much property, such countless family fortunes were dependent, directly and indirectly, on the maintenance of slavery that it seemed at first impossible that Parliament, itself much in need of reform, could ever be persuaded to abolish it, for over four-fifths of Britain's revenue from overseas trade came from the sugar islands.

In some years as many as 100,000 Africans were transported, and their cause received great publicity in the 1770s from two legal decisions, one in England and the other in Scotland. There were perhaps as many as 50,000 negroes in England, most of them in service with families that had interests in the West Indies. They sometimes ran away from their masters and in 1772 one of them, James Somerset, was seized and was about to be shipped back to his owner's plantation when a comparatively poor business man named Granville Sharp (1735-1813), who had made himself a legal expert, intervened. Sharp's arguments against applying the law of property disturbed the judge, a Scot educated in England, William Murray, Lord Mansfield (1705-1793), yet his sentence was: 'The air of England has long been too pure for a slave, and every man is free who breathes it. Every man who comes to England is entitled to the protection of English law, whatever oppression he may have suffered, and whatever may be the colour of his skin. Let the negro Somerset be discharged.'

The case in Scotland, according to James Boswell, the biographer of Dr Johnson, who approved of slavery while his hero detested it, 'went upon much broader ground than the case of Somerset'. A negro named Joseph Knight, who had been enslaved in West Africa, bought in Jamaica and taken to Scotland by his master, was persuaded by abolitionists to bring an action claiming his liberty. The great majority of the Lords of Session decided for him; four, including the President, against; and Knight was declared free.

It was frequently argued that the slavers by employing so many seamen provided 'a nursery for the Royal Navy'. This fallacy was exposed by Thomas Clarkson (1760-1846), a Cambridge graduate in mathematics who devoted the whole of his long life to the abolitionist cause and deserves to be ranked as high as Wilberforce. His energy and persistence were beyond praise. He once went in search of a witness who had seen a particularly revolting example of slaving methods in West Africa and had subsequently joined the Navy. On a tour of naval ports he went on board over 260 warships before finding his man. In the taverns and inns of Bristol and Liverpool where ships obtained their crews Clarkson would sit in the corner watching; he soon found that most of the captains of slavers had such reputations for cruelty that they could scarcely get men, however much money they offered, unless they first made them helpless with drink. These nurseries of the Navy were in fact torture-chambers and often death traps.

Another invaluable witness was the Reverend John Newton (1725-1807), rector of St Mary Woolnoth, London, a friend of the poet William Cowper. As a young man he had been the captain of a slaver for nine years, and then experienced a religious conversion. It was from him that Wilberforce learned one of the most powerful of the arguments he used in the House of Commons: 'We depend on the vices of African princes for the very maintenance of the Slave Trade. Does the King of Barbessia want brandy? He has only to send his troops in the night time to burn and desolate a village. The captives will serve as commodities that may be bartered with the British trader.'

This abhorrence of slave-raiding struck the African kings who supplied slaves as most amusing. King Pepple, whose dominions lay on the Bonny river, was, when sober, exceptionally intelligent, and kept himself informed about the proceedings of the British Parliament. He asked how many men had been killed in the recent battles in Europe, and when he was told, roared with laughter, saying: 'What wo wo palaver you make!' (What silly talk).

After the outbreak of the Revolution in France an abolitionist committee was formed there, Les Amis des Noirs, and Clarkson went to Paris to concert action with them. Les Amis included Mirabeau, Lafayette, and the Abbé Grégoire, who brought before the National Assembly a law giving coloured people the right of citizenship. Robespierre, speaking in support, declared: 'Let the colonies perish if they must cost you your honour and justice.' When the news of the new law reached Saint-Domingue, France's richest West Indian colony, there was a terrible revolt. Negroes, drunk with rum and the heady slogans of the Revolution, succeeded by murder, rape and arson in gaining command of the whole island. Their leader, Toussaint L'Ouverture, negotiated as monarch of the island with its former rulers. In 1800 Bonaparte, whose wife belonged to Saint-Domingue, sent out an army which made an unsuccessful attempt to reconquer the colony. By fraud they captured Toussaint and sent him to an Alpine prison where he died. In Britain the massacre of French planters ended hopes of abolition for the next sixteen years. None could contest the argument that it was politically unsafe to free slaves.

132

CHAPTER ELEVEN

The Nineteenth Century

The Monarchy

George III	1760-1820
George IV	
Prince Regent	1811-1820
King	1820-1830
William IV	1830-1837
Victoria	1837-1901

Victory over the French

In 1802, after nine years of war, peace was signed at Amiens between Britain and France. It was, in Sheridan's words, 'a peace everybody was glad of and nobody proud of'. The British restored to France, Spain and Holland all the colonial territories they had captured except Trinidad and Ceylon. Napoleon, as First Consul, welcomed a temporary peace as an opportunity for transforming the civil administration of the country. His system made France the most conservative and insular of European states for the next century and a half. Soon, however, Napoleon's restless ambition had provoked a fresh war. In retaliation for the seizure by the navy of some French ships Napoleon ordered the internment of twelve thousand British travellers in France. These he held for eleven years. In 1804 he crowned himself Emperor of the French, and in the following year assembled an army at Boulogne for the invasion of England. This project required that the French fleet with their Spanish allies should drive the British out of the Channel.

The Spanish and French ships were bigger than the British and carried more heavy guns, but they were not so manoeuvreable and their bases were too far from the Channel. The British could slip in and out of Portsmouth and Plymouth in most weather conditions and since they held Gibraltar, could watch the Atlantic harbours of Spain. In asking his admirals to elude Nelson, Napoleon forgot that he could not command the wind. In September he abandoned invasion plans and sent his army eastward to attack the Austrians on the upper Danube, where they took 50,000 prisoners. In December Napoleon's victory at Austerlitz was so complete that the Austrians sued for peace.

The annihilation of the French and Spanish fleets at Trafalgar on 21 October 1805 came after the danger of immediate invasion had passed but it removed the risk of a

GOD save the KING.

Doublons.

SPANISH Dollar Bag Consigned to Boney.

My LADS, The rest of the GALLEONS with the TREASURE from LA PLATA, are waiting half loaded at CARTAGENA, for the arrival of those from PERU at PANAMA, as soon as that takes place, they are to sail for PORTOVELO, to take in the rest of their Cargo, with Provisions and Water for the Voyage to EUROPE. They stay at PORTO-VELO a few days only. Such a Chance perhaps will never occur again,

THE FLYING
PALLAS,
Of 36 GUNS,
At PLYMOUTH,

is a new and uncommonly fine Frigate. Built on purpose. And ready for an EXPEDITION, as soon as some more good Hands are on board;

Captain Lord Cochrane,

(who was not drowned in the ARAB as reported) Commands her. The sooner you are on board the better.

None need apply, but SEAMEN, or Stout Hands, able to rouse about the Field Pieces, and carry an hundred weight of PEWTER, without stopping, at least three Miles.

COCHRANE.

To British Seamen.

BONEY's CORONATION
Is postponed for want of COBBS.

J. BARFIELD, Printer, Wardour-Street.

Rendezvous, at the White Flag,

A naval recruiting poster. Lord Cochrane was planning to attack a Spanish fleet, since Spain was a reluctant ally of 'Boney', who crowned himself Emperor of the French in 1804. Later Lord Cochrane helped to liberate the South American colonies of Spain. Life at sea was hard, but a chance of plunder made it attractive to the adventurous. 'Cobbs', a word sometimes used for 'ore', is slang for gold

further attempt. Pitt had hoped that the Austrians might complete Napoleon's downfall. They had been part of the Grand Alliance which he had engineered and financed, intending they they should combine forces with the Prussians and Russians, but these doubtful allies failed to reach the battlefield of Austerlitz on time. By 1807 Napoleon had defeated them each separately.

The French now conceived the idea that they could ruin the British, 'a nation of shop-keepers', to use Napoleon's crude phrase, by closing all the ports of Europe to British ships. Only Spain and Portugal remained out of their control. In 1808, under pretext of liberating the Spaniards from a corrupt monarchy, the French marched on Madrid.

The Spanish army was, as Napoleon knew, 'pour rire'. Spanish patriotism he did not even try to conciliate and the French army treated the people with insolent cruelty. For the next four years guerrilla warfare with atrocity and counter-atrocity ensued, a time of horror recorded for posterity in the paintings of Goya. In 1809 Napoleon himself went to Madrid, intent on overrunning Portugal. In Lisbon the British had put Sir John Moore in command. His methods of training had already transformed the army and now he gave it an example of great daring. With bad weather due he marched towards Bayonne, hoping to cut the French off, or, if that proved too difficult, to retreat towards the coast and meet the fleet at Corunna. Napoleon abandoned the invasion of Portugal, and chased north after the British, marching with his men at twenty miles a day through the snowy mountains. Moore, with one French army in front of him and Napoleon behind, had to make for Corunna. In a fighting mid-winter retreat he saved his army, but lost his life.

The Peninsular War now began to drain the French empire of some of its best troops. Moore's successor, Sir Arthur Wellesley, later Duke of Wellington, campaigned for over four years, creating out of limited resources an excellent headquarters staff and an infantry force which destroyed the legend that the French were invincible. In 1812 he liberated Madrid, but was compelled to conduct a long retreat to the Portuguese border at the very time that Napoleon's army was retreating from Moscow. He re-entered Spain the next year and by 1814 had fought his way into the south of France, where he won the last battle of the war before news of Napoleon's abdication reached him.

After his fall from power Napoleon, who had been deserted by almost all his army chiefs, including Marshal Ney, was sent to the island of Elba. He was, however, not kept under surveillance, and escaped to France in March 1815. Marshal Ney rejoined him and soon Napoleon was marching north with a large force on Brussels. Wellington had been appointed to command in Belgium a hastily assembled British army, much inferior to the one that had done so well in Spain. He also had contingents from Germany and the Netherlands. The Prussian army under Marshal Blücher, operating independently, was forced to retreat before the battle of Waterloo began, but returned to take part in the final phase and in the pursuit that ended all Napoleon's hopes.

The victory had shown the superiority of British over French tactics. Marshal Ney, deputising for the emperor, who took little part in directing the battle, sent massed columns—the old French revolutionary style of attack—against the British line and later cavalry against the infantry squares, but the steadiness and discipline of Wellington's men, and his presence wherever the danger was greatest, ensured that the line was never broken. There was nothing, however, inevitable about the result. A large part of the Duke's staff had either been killed or severely wounded, and from every regiment there were long lists of casualties. Wellington, one of the most undemonstrative of men, wept when he read them.

Parliament and Reform

To 'free-born Englishmen', as the men of 1815 were fond of calling themselves, the ideals which the French Revolution had proclaimed but never achieved—liberty, equality and fraternity—no longer appeared, as they did on the continent, dangerous. The British constitution had proved its strength and had contributed to the downfall of Napoleon. As Pitt had predicted just before his death in 1806, Britain had saved herself by her exertions and Europe by her example. Yet the British delegates at the Congress of Vienna, Lord Castlereagh and the Duke of Wellington, met with the jealousy and dislike usually experienced by those who have conferred a benefit. At home Wilberforce and the abolitionists were insisting that the Congress should declare the slave trade illegal, as Britain had done in 1807; this was regarded as one more display of British hypocrisy aimed at rivals in the sugar trade who might benefit from their philanthropy. The duke, for his part, considered the abolitionists importunate, and wished to concentrate on preventing a French recovery, knowing that the allies, by restoring Louis XVIII and his revengeful family, had done nothing to salve the pride of a defeated nation. It was also easy to pass laws against the trade but quite another matter to make them effective. The British, with the only navy capable of patrolling two thousand miles of African coastline under sail, found the task of enforcement beyond their strength. The chief powers eventually agreed to laws against slaving, but it continued under various flags until the American Civil War put an end to slavery in the southern states.

The abolitionists in the United Kingdom were only one of many groups who began to use extra-Parliamentary pressure on post-war governments. Their techniques of agitation were imitated by radicals in their demands for Parliamentary reform. Pitt would have acted in the 1790s but was prevented by the war. He knew that commercial interests were much under-represented. Some places, once quite small, had grown into thriving industrial towns yet remained without representation except through the counties. Wilberforce, for example, a citizen of Hull, was for many years returned for the county of Yorkshire. Many other county seats returned unopposed candidates chosen by local landowners, but in Yorkshire voters, coming to poll by show of hands in the county town, some by road and some by river, crowded into York Minster for the customary service. When asked what party they would vote for they proudly said: 'For Wilberforce, of course!'

The county franchise was uniform, and the voters mainly from the middle class, but in the boroughs it showed every kind of variety. In fifty-three of them it was extremely wide; in some, all able-bodied males had the vote, provided they were not in receipt of relief, and were able 'to keep their pot boiling', that is, provide themselves with the necessities of life. These 'potwallopers' were the envy of radicals in other boroughs, and gave them an excellent argument for a reform act that would grant universal manhood suffrage. Such 'democracy' was anathema to the Whigs, whose leader, Earl Grey, now an old man, had advocated reform before the war. A leading Tory, Sir Robert Peel, arguing against any change, pleaded that in Lancashire the moderate redistribution of seats proposed by the Whigs would deprive working people of the vote, but there were so many scandalous abuses in the so-called 'rotten boroughs', where only a handful were entitled to vote, that reform was generally accepted, except by the House of Lords. There opposition to the Whigs, particularly from the most distinguished of all the peers, the Duke of Wellington, was resented throughout the country. In Nottingham mobs burnt down the castle. In Bristol all the more important buildings in the centre of the town were set on fire. Such violence was possible because there were no police forces outside London, where Sir Robert Peel's blue-coats, first mustered under Act of Parliament in 1829, kept the capital free from trouble.

The cherished liberty of free assembly often led not only to political riots but to the smashing of weaving looms and farm threshing machines by armed mobs. Such experiences were common enough for business men who could expect no compensation and had to rely on their own personal courage to defend their property. When the troops were called out, and a few offenders caught, punishment was extremely severe; even boys were hanged and hundreds were transported to Australia. To many of those who had lived through the French Revolution of 1789, read the news from Paris of the deposition of Charles X in 1830, and knew that labourers were robbing farmers and burning corn stacks all through the southern counties, it seemed that Britain too was on the verge of revolution.

Yet the unreformed House of Commons proved an adequate safety-valve for the many discontents of a rapidly swelling population (8,900,000 at the first census in 1801 rising to 13,900,000 in 1831). The Duke of Wellington, who had been born in Dublin, realised that for Ireland Catholic Emancipation, that is the removal of all the disabilities preventing Catholics from taking up political careers, was necessary if civil war were to be avoided, and forced George IV to give his consent to it in 1829. From then on the affairs of Ireland, where the countryside was one of the most poverty-stricken and back-ward in Europe, continued intermittently for nearly ninety years to bedevil the processes of Parliament, while Irish members extorted, first from one party and then from the other, promises to remedy evils which were beyond human power to cure.

The reformed House of Commons which met in 1833 did not, in spite of the redistribu-tion of about 100 seats, differ greatly in composition from its predecessors. The electorate in England and Wales had been increased from 217,000 voters to 435,000, and, in 1867, on the eve of the next reform, the continuing rise in population had increased it to over a million, but there was no payment for members and voters chose much the same kind of candidates as before. There was still plenty of bribery, corruption and intimidation by landlords, since there was no secret ballot until after 1872. Only a small part of the nation interested itself in politics. In the five general elections between 1832 and 1847 only about half the seats were contested. The new House of Commons contained 217 sons of peers and baronets; in 1865 the number was 180; and throughout the century the influence of the House of Lords, where most seats were held by hereditary right, was very great. None the less legislation proceeded at a creditable speed and in the decade 1833 to 1843 the administration of the Poor Law was reorganised on uniform national lines; the new towns were given considerable rights of self-government; and conditions of employment in industry were brought under some elementary control. This dull work, carried out in a harsh, ungenerous spirit, deeply disappointed the radicals who had done so much to push the Whigs into the 1832 reform. A great popular agitation was set on foot mainly in London and the northern counties for a Charter granting true liberty to the people. This attracted mostly manual workers including many displaced hand-loom weavers. Chartist propaganda made six demands: (1) universal manhood suffrage; (2) equal electoral districts; (3) removal of property qualifications for members of Parliament; (4) payment of members of Parliament; (5) secret ballot; and (6) annual general elections. In support of them a million signatures were collected on a petition which was taken to Westminster with great ceremony. It was then found that many of the signatures collected in the streets and at public meetings were bogus, and in 1848 the movement collapsed. It had attempted to do too much too quickly. The British instinct was for piecemeal reform, and in the course of the next hundred years all but the last of the Six Points became law.

The railway legislation of Parliament in the 1840s could not be based on long experience like that on the electoral laws. The popular economic theory of the time held that there

Chester-Holyhead Railway at Penmaen Mawr. A special embankment had to be made to protect the track against storm waves and a tunnel blasted through the mountain side for 230 yards. In some parts the track had to be covered as a protection against rock falls.

138

Construction of the tube for the main span of the Britannia bridge, 1849. This method of building a bridge, here used to carry the Chester-Holyhead railway over the Menai Strait, was invented by Robert Stephenson. The bridge, opened in 1850, had four spans, two of 460 feet over water, and these were floated into position on pontoons. The Admiralty had insisted that ships must be able to pass freely underneath

should be no interference in such private enterprises as the new railways. Yet the companies were buying up land in all directions to build lines. The phenomenal success of the passenger service between Liverpool and Manchester, a line opened in 1830 and using Stephenson locomotives, was at first considered to be exceptional because it was short and connected two populous towns. The idea for example of a London-Birmingham line, 112 miles long, seemed exceedingly ambitious. George Stephenson (1781-1848), whose early work on colliery engines and railways had been backed by wealthy Quaker business men, had no qualms. He argued the case for new lines before Parliamentary committees, puzzling members with his broad Northumbrian accent but convincing them by his sturdy common sense and self-confidence in face of hostile questions. Yet the railway engineers were the servants of the companies, seldom investors; shareholders were numerous and scattered, and the directors often pre-occupied with other matters. The first of many gigantic impersonal industrial organisations had arrived. Making railways pay was a new business with no precedents, and Parliament was afraid that high monopoly fares might be charged. Shareholders risked enormous sums of money, and in 1848 speculation brought disaster to many. Yet the Government feared to insist on a national scheme drawn up to link the ironfields, coalmines, textile towns and ports in a logical way. Different companies were allowed to build separate unconnected terminuses near city centres, a costly waste of effort, since passengers and goods had to find other means of transport from one terminus to another. The surroundings of railway stations became notorious for their grimy appearance and foggy atmosphere, though this was caused as much by the chimneys of the new mills and factories sited along the lines as by the coal-fired steam locomotives.

Action to preserve the beauty of old cities proved too difficult, but on passenger safety and many other matters the State did intervene, fixing limits for fares and freight charges, and prescribing slow 'Parliamentary' trains which stopped at every station to comply with the law and held up express services using the same track. Legislative errors in such novel circumstances were inevitable, but when they have all been catalogued, the achievements of the railway men still command unlimited admiration. Samuel Smiles, the biographer of the Stephensons, wrote in 1862 of the London to Birmingham line, completed in 1838: 'The work was performed by about 20,000 men in less than five years ... in the face of every conceivable obstruction and difficulty by a company of private individuals out of their own resources without the aid of Government or the contribution of one farthing of public money.'

A generation later, in 1867, the Tory Disraeli's first cabinet, after many hesitations, extended the franchise to the better-off working men in the towns. This doubled the size of the electorate in Great Britain, bringing it to 2,225,000, or about one in three of the adult male population. A *Punch* cartoon of the time called this 'a leap in the dark', so convinced were politicians that politics were of absorbing interest, and that the new voters would be a prey to revolutionary enthusiasms. The next year Disraeli's party was voted out, and the Liberal leader, William Gladstone, became Prime Minister for the first time, remaining in office until 1874, and introducing a large number of reforms. Tories affected to regard him as a demagogue, and it seemed that their worst fears about extending the franchise were being fulfilled. His ministry made entrance to the civil service, hitherto in the gift of politicians, subject to a competitive examination; put an end to the purchase of commissions in the Army; reorganised the infantry regiments on a territorial county basis; and took the first steps towards making elementary education compulsory.

The next alterations in the electoral system enacted by Gladstone's second administration (1880–1885) were the most radical of the whole century. The total electorate in Great Britain was brought up to about 5,000,000 from 2,500,000, that is, about two in three of the adult male population. Before this Redistribution of Seats Act (1885) a Corrupt and Illegal Practices Prevention Act (1883) had set a limit to the amount candidates might spend on elections by paying agents, free entertainment and other devices. The old two-member boroughs were broken up and single-member constituencies of roughly equal size created, the boundaries being drawn artificially without regard to historic associations. The new divisions were so big that personal contact between candidates and the bulk of the electorate became very difficult and only after a member had sat for many years did he become well-known in his division.

New spheres of popular government were opened up in 1888 and 1894. Elected county councils and some 6,000 parish councils were established. These were for a long time dominated by the Conservative party whose country members proved willing to devote themselves to local government work which was unpaid, repetitive and dull. Among Liberals Lord Rosebery, a youthful peer and a most talented speaker and writer, set an example by serving as Chairman of the London County Council.

Unmarried women were given the right to vote in county council elections in 1888 and to stand as candidates on the same terms as men. In 1894 these rights were extended to married women. This was the first result of a long campaign led by women who had won high academic honours at those universities to whose examinations they had been admitted. Yet the Liberal and Conservative parties remained firm against allowing female suffrage in Parliamentary elections. This illogicality was based on an irrational fear that women might take over the political world. When, in the next century, women were granted equal political rights, few were willing to make the sacrifice of normal social life required of those who follow political careers.

The two parties drew their support from quite different areas. The Liberals were strong in Scotland—both Gladstone and his successor Lord Rosebery were of Scottish descent; in Ireland, where the Nationalists wished Gladstone's plans for Home Rule to succeed; in Wales, where the Nonconformists were usually Radicals; in the northern manufacturing districts of England; and in London. The Conservatives commanded the country districts and market towns lying to the east and south of a line from the Humber to the Bristol Channel.

All the electoral reforms of the 1880s and 1890s were strongly opposed by the House of Lords, where the overwhelming majority lacked the imagination to see that the extension of the franchise in the country areas would benefit Conservatives rather than the Liberals. The Lords even opposed the creation of parish councils and the Liberal government, to get the Bill passed, were required to restrict the councils' powers by limiting their income to the proceeds of a 3d rate. Gladstone, in one of his last speeches in Parliament, declared that the opposition of the Lords to the will of the Commons could not be allowed to continue. The constitution was thus in as unsteady a state after the extension of the franchise as before, and Britain stood in danger of single-chamber government based on universal suffrage, that is, the most tyrannous form of democracy known to history.

Children, Work and Schooling

On 4 July 1840 Lord Ashley, a Tory member of the House of Commons, later better known as Lord Shaftesbury, wrote in his diary: 'Anxious, very anxious about my sweeps [climbing boys]; the Conservative(!) Peers threaten fierce oppostion and the radical Ministers warmly support the Bill. Normanby [Lord Normanby, Home Secretary in Lord Melbourne's second government] has been manly, open, kind-hearted and firm.

I shall have no ease or pleasure in the recess, should these poor children be despised by the Lords and tossed to the mercy of their savage purchasers. I find that Evangelical religionists are not those on whom I can rely.' Ashley had become famous for his support of legislation to prevent the use of young children in industry, but had not previously concerned himself with the sufferings of the climbing boys apprenticed to, or, as he wrote, purchased by, sweeps and sent up house chimneys to clean them with hand-brushes. Oliver Twist, the hero of Charles Dickens's novel of that name, first published in 1838, narrowly escapes being legally apprenticed to a sweep.

Opposition to the prevention of this practice arose from the exaggerated fear of property-owners that fires caused by soot-choked flues might destroy their homes and possessions. There was no public fire service, even in towns, though some insurance companies maintained private services which attended fires in houses which their clients had marked with the company badge in metal. There was also apprehension that if laws were made against climbing boys there could be no objection in principle to further interference with the practices of other trades. One peer declared that all such reforms should be left 'entirely to the moral feelings of the most moral people on the face of the earth'.

Members of the Commons had made attempts to prohibit the use of climbing boys since 1817, but they had all been baulked by the House of Lords. A law passed in 1834 had forbidden the use of boys under ten, but those over that age were too big to enter chimneys, and there was no means of protecting younger children. In 1840 the government proposed that climbing by any person under twenty-one and apprenticing to sweeps of any boy under sixteen should be forbidden. The evidence submitted of cruelty by master-sweeps to their boys was so frightful that the bill was passed, and many owners of large houses had their chimneys rebuilt to allow the use of mechanical brooms, among them the Duke of Wellington, who did not approve of the Act but was scrupulous in obeying it.

Yet in the next twelve years evidence accumulated that in many parts of the country the law was being ignored. As the government was pre-occupied with the Crimean War (1854-1856), it refused to consider fresh legislation. In 1861 Shaftesbury had the sweeps included under the investigations of the Children's Employment Commission, but not until 1875, when one more child had been 'killed in action', did Parliament hit upon an effective device for enforcement. A new Act made it illegal to run a sweep's business without a magistrate's licence, and this could be refused to applicants known to have broken the law.

Chimney-sweeping was by no means the only trade which had adapted the medieval apprenticeship system to the purchase of free labour. The poor had large families and often died young, leaving their orphaned children to the care of the workhouses, where they were supported out of the rates. The financial advantage to be gained by selling them as apprentices to mill and factory owners was too tempting. This kind of enslavement occurring near at hand did not upset the conscience or arouse the compassion of Evangelicals as negro slavery had done, but it continued to stir Ashley, who during a wretchedly unhappy childhood had absorbed from a nursemaid the Protestant beliefs that gave force and fervour to his public life. After a happy marriage he devoted himself to the cause of women and children and when he died in 1885 the poor followed his funeral procession through the streets of London.

His first big success came after a journey through the mining districts. In 1842 a commission, appointed by Parliament and consisting of a doctor, an economist and two factory inspectors, published its report on the working conditions of women and children in the mines. Public opinion was horrified by its revelations of physically degrading labour carried out in wet, dark mineshafts. In every district except North Staffordshire, where the younger children earned better wages in the potteries, the employment of children under seven was common. Some miners carried babies down the mine to scare rats away from their snacks of food. That in the hot conditions underground men and women worked together stripped to the waist upset members of the House of Commons more than any other piece of information.

Ashley at once introduced a Bill prohibiting the employment of women and girls below ground and restricting the age of entry for boys to thirteen. He had the good fortune to speak shortly after an attempt to assassinate the queen while she was driving in London and the nearness to death of a young wife and mother had brought a sense of reality into the House. His arguments were so eloquent that Richard Cobden, a representative of the manufacturers' interests and a leader of the current agitation for the repeal of the Corn Laws, to which Sir Robert Peel's government was opposed, crossed the floor of the House, took his hand and said: 'You know how opposed I have been to your views, but I don't think I have ever been put into such a frame of mind in the whole course of my life as I have been by your speech.'

In the Upper House things were very different; Lord Londonderry reminded their lordships that over ten million pounds were invested in the mines of Northumberland and Durham alone, and that the education which the philanthropists intended to give the boys hitherto employed would destroy 'the equilibrium of society'. His colliery manager, John Buddle, had told him 'of the superior advantages of a practical education in collieries to a reading education'; after the age of ten boys did not 'acquire those habits that are particularly necessary to enable them to perform work in the mines'. Their lordships agreed, and Mr Buddle was sent to Ashley and persuaded him to make ten instead of thirteen the age of entry for boys.

The London street urchins whom Ashley studied could, he felt, only escape from a life of poverty and crime if they were taught to read and write. At night they slept under arches, in porches and on roof tops, and for them he founded 'Ragged Schools' paid for by his friends. By 1849 he was able to tell the House of Commons that there were 82 such schools with 124 paid and 929 voluntary teachers and 8,000 pupils. Eighteen years later the numbers had nearly trebled. By then the teaching of the poor provided by voluntary effort was not considered sufficient. Two societies, one sponsored by the Church of England and the other by the Nonconformists, had set up elementary schools both in towns and villages. Nominal fees were charged and the chief educational aim was to put an end to illiteracy while at the same time familiarising the children with the Gospels and the creeds of church and chapel. Shaftesbury typified many Evangelicals in opposing rate-aided education on the ground that it would be 'a water-rate to extinguish religious fire among young people'.

In 1858 a government commission headed by the Duke of Newcastle reported that only about 4·5 per cent of children under eleven were not attending school, but recommended that local boards should be set up to raise educational standards by relating the amount of aid given to schools out of public funds to their efficiency as judged by tests and inspectors' examinations. Payment by results was an excellent idea, provided that it was in the hands of men such as Matthew Arnold (1822-1888), who combined his work as a school inspector with the life of a poet and critic and once defined culture as 'acquainting ourselves with the best that has been known and said in the world and thus with the history of the human spirit'. Unfortunately he, like many educated Englishmen of his day, was an admirer of Prussia. The complete victories so unexpectedly won by the Prussian army over the Austrian empire in 1866 and the French empire in 1870 were attributed to the efficiency of their school system and not to the ineptitude of the statesmen and unpreparedness of the generals who had opposed them.

When Gladstone came to power in 1868, he appointed a Quaker, W. E. Forster, vice-president of the committee of the Privy Council on education. In 1870 Forster pushed through Parliament a bill for non-sectarian rate-aided schools to supplement the church-

St Dunstan's College, a school built on the southern outskirts of London in 1888. The building, which cost £35,000, was provided out of charitable funds accumulated by a City church, St Dunstan-in-the-East. It charged fees of £8 to £16 a year to educate 400 boys from 8 to 17 years of age for 'manufacturing, commercial and professional pursuits, special attention being paid to scientific, technical and commercial education'

Sokol, the first ship to attain a speed of 30 knots. A destroyer for the Imperial Russian navy, this was the first warship to be constructed of high-tensile steel, a lighter material than the mild steel previously used. Built at Poplar on the Thames by Messrs. Yarrow, a firm that later moved to Clydeside, it was fitted with eight of the firm's patent water-tube boilers

aided schools. The figures he used for illiteracy were based on uniquely bad conditions in Manchester, Liverpool and Birmingham, where existing schools had been unable to provide any education for the children of immigrants who had flooded in from Ireland. The new schools charged small fees except for children whose parents were judged to be destitute. In this way the English, in spite of their long tradition of personal freedom, were committed to a system of State education, devised in conscious emulation of the Prussians, by a Quaker who had been caught in the general admiration for the discipline of 'a nation-in-arms'. Yet in order to limit State expenditure, a constant objective of Gladstone's statesmanship, payment by results was allowed to become a harsh and mechanical routine. Fortunately no attempt at uniformity had much chance of success. The educational world (it did not deserve to be called a system) remained a jungle in which Anglicans quarrelled with Nonconformists and a rapidly growing Roman Catholic community, while each in jealous emulation of the other poured private funds into a host of schools, colleges and extra-mural university lectureships.

Few leading scientists and inventors owed anything to school or university. Charles Darwin (1800-1882) showed no particular aptitude for learning at school or college, but, as a single-handed recluse, worked out from his world-wide travels the biological principles of Natural Selection and the Survival of the Fittest, principles which statesmen ignorantly upheld to justify the Prussian policy of 'blood and iron'. Sir Henry Bessemer (1813-1895), the inventor of a process for making cheap steel that revolutionised British industry, built his own workshops. Sidney Gilchrist Thomas (1850-1885), who adapted

Bessemer's invention to the smelting of phosphoric ores, did his experiments in the backyard of a small suburban house, and in a similar setting William Crush (1850-1914) started work for Alfred Yarrow on his firm's water tube-boilers. Eight of these, installed in the destroyer Sokol in 1895, enabled the Imperial Russian navy to be the first to have a vessel that could travel at 30 knots. Sir Joseph Wilson Swan (1828-1914), who, like Crush, had left school at the age of twelve, demonstrated to the Newcastle Chemical Society an incandescent electric lamp of his invention a year before Edison's first success in the USA.

In Scotland the universities took a much greater part in scientific progress. At Edinburgh Sir James Simpson (1811-1870) in the 1840s carried out successful experiments in the use of chloroform in surgery, then mainly a matter of amputation with a high death rate from wound infection. Precautions against this were suggested by the Professor of Surgery at Glasgow University, Dr Joseph Lister, afterwards Lord Lister (1827-1912), who had studied Pasteur's discoveries and at once applied them in his operating theatre, first by antiseptic and then by aseptic methods which dramatically reduced the death rate among his cases. Without Lord Kelvin (1824-1907), also a professor at Glasgow, electrical engineering would have made little advance, and without the Edinburgh mathematician Clerk-Maxwell's work at Cambridge the splitting of the atom would have been impossible. Thus the two nations combined to make the reign of Victoria, in spite of all the evil by-products of industry, a time of progress and enlightenment.

The Empire, the Army and the Navy

The governments that re-drew the political map of Europe in 1815 were, apart from the British, little interested in the affairs of other continents. Metternich, the Chancellor of the Austrian Empire, said when he heard of the Greek revolt against the Turkish empire: 'Let it burn itself out beyond the pale of civilisation.' It was his proud assumption that civilisation stopped on Austria's eastern border.

The British government was self-centred in another way. They regarded any nation seeking to win independence from foreign autocracy as a convert in need of assistance. Warships helped the Spanish colonies in South America to break away from the motherland. A fleet was sent to the Peloponnese and, in conjunction with French and Russian squadrons, destroyed the Egyptian navy that the Sultan was employing to suppress the Greek rebellion.

Such exploits enabled the Royal Navy to retain the popularity that it had won under Nelson. The army on the other hand was forgotten and neglected. Its commander-in-chief, the Duke of Wellington, set his face against all change and improvement, even defending the practice of duelling and allowing the service to be starved of everything that might have made soldiering an attractive profession. Barracks were places of revolting squalor, where life was more degrading than in prison; flogging was the punishment for even minor offences; and long service engagement kept the men away from home and almost all civilising influences. The duke scattered them in small contingents all over the world with the result that the officers received little training in army manoeuvres or battle tactics except in India.

146

The nation had to pay the price for this ungrateful treatment when war came. In the meantime the House of Commons, dominated by men whose chief interest was manufacturing and trade, had no wish to invest in the empire, asserting that as soon as colonies prospered they would want to declare their independence, as the Americans had done. Nevertheless, a small minority of men believed that Britain could and should become the centre of a world-wide empire, among whom were Sir Stamford Raffles (1781-1826), the founder of Singapore; Edward Gibbon Wakefield (1796-1862), who promoted colonies in South Australia and New Zealand; and Sir George Grey (1812-1898), who served in Australia, New Zealand and South Africa. Their achievements, won in face of general indifference, caused little change of heart in Whitehall. Neither the Horse Guards (as the War Office was called) nor the Admiralty modified their traditional methods to meet the strategic needs of 'Britain overseas'. There was no joint planning staff and no one Minister to take responsibility for imperial defence.

Foreign affairs were, like those of the Empire, conducted throughout the century with little thought for military consequences. National pride and ambition demanded that Britain, as the leading industrial nation in the world, should make its voice heard in every international crisis, and the men to feed this arrogant spirit were not slow to push themselves forward. The first to succeed in this was Lord Palmerston. He was in charge of foreign policy from 1830 to 1841 and again from 1848 to 1852, and popularised the idea that the Russian empire would in some way harm British interests if it were allowed to dominate the affairs of Turkey and Egypt, both countries where the priests of the Moslem religion, themselves ignorant and backward, had so strong a hold on the population that only the most ruthless and autocratic Sultans could make their will obeyed. Palmerston, though posing on most other occasions as the champion of constitutional liberty, cared nothing for the Turkish people or their religion as long as he could use them as a barrier against the power of Russia. Communications between Britain and the British forces in India passed through Egypt, and he found it easy to persuade his political friends that even at the risk of war the southward drive of the Russians must be stopped.

Playing with threats produced at last the disaster of the Crimean War (1854-1856), in which Britain allied herself with France, Turkey and Piedmont to thwart the Tsar, Nicholas I. A military display without casualties would have suited these ill-assorted allies, especially the ramshackle Empire of Napoleon III. The British and French armies, each under elderly commanders who were physically unfit for active service, were sent first to Bulgaria and then, too late in the season, to the Crimea.

The Russians, with incredible inefficiency, allowed them to land unopposed. The allies' first engagement was a victory and their objective, the Russian naval base at Sebastopol, could have been captured at once if the commanders had agreed on hot pursuit. A long winter campaign, several indecisive battles and a costly siege ensued before Sebastopol was taken and the war ended. The discipline and courage of British troops had been fully displayed in face of enormous odds, but nothing could conceal from the nation or the world the organisational weakness and tactical incompetence of their generals.

Within a year the army was put to another test by the Indian Mutiny. Entire British communities in Bengal and northern India were massacred and the government almost overthrown by rebellious native troops. An electric telegraph, then a new invention, connecting the government in Calcutta with the besieged garrison in Delhi was kept open long enough for help to be summoned from the Punjab and from overseas. After desperate fighting and some terrible reprisals order was restored.

The superiority of the British in these two conflicts was due to a new weapon. Since the death of the Duke of Wellington the infantry had at last abandoned smooth-bore muzzle-loading muskets in favour of rifles with greased paper cartridges. These were still muzzle-loaded, but volley-firing became more rapid and more accurate. In most respects, however, drill and tactics, the magnificent but impractical uniforms and showy accoutrements, favoured by Napoleon I and imitated by all European armies, were little changed.

For twenty years after the Crimean War the Russians, frustrated in the south, advanced to the east, threatening the British Empire in India, and reaching the Pacific at Vladivostok. Yet the Slav subjects of Turkey continued to agitate for the national independence which the Greeks and Rumanians had already won. In Bulgaria a guerrilla movement sought to detach the country from the Turkish empire. The Sultan sent an ill-disciplined force of Bashi-Bazouks to deal with this incipient revolt. They massacred guilty and innocent alike to the number of 12,000. Reports of this reached the London Liberal newspaper, the *Daily News*, before they reached Disraeli, the Prime Minister. Gladstone, an Opposition leader, seized upon the news to go on a speaking tour in Midlothian, using all his eloquence to demand that the Sultan should be punished by expulsion from Europe. No statesman had discussed foreign affairs in public in this way before. His conservative critics rightly regarded it as a most dangerous precedent. The Russians were more practical than Gladstone; they declared war on the Turks and, after some difficulty, one of their armies reached the neighbourhood of Constantinople. The Sultan made peace, consenting to the creation of a Russian-occupied Bulgaria reaching to the Aegean coast. The other governments of Europe refused to recognise such a settlement and a European Congress met in Berlin. Disraeli and Lord Salisbury, with the help of Bismarck, Chancellor of the German Empire created seven years before, persuaded the Russians to accept a smaller Bulgaria. The Austrians, who had 'liberated' the Bosnians from Turkish rule during the war, were allowed to incorporate them in their polyglot Empire. The German drive to the east had begun, and the scene had been set for the opening phase of the Great War. It was a strange result for Gladstone to have achieved.

In the last twenty years of the century the overseas expansion of the nations of western Europe produced a chain of disputes and steadily increasing friction especially over African affairs. The British, who had quarrelled with the Boers in Cape Colony earlier over their oppressive treatment of coloured peoples, had far more knowledge and experience of Africa than their rivals, thanks to explorers such as Mungo Park on the Niger, Livingstone on the Zambesi and among the great lakes, and Speke on the sources of the Nile. In British South Africa Cecil Rhodes, who had become a diamond

Winston Churchill at the age of 24. He is wearing the uniform of a Hussar, having, after much opposition from its commander, joined the army with which Kitchener defeated the Khalifa at Omdurman in the Sudan in 1898

millionaire in the first diggings at Kimberley, extended his operations on to Boer territory when gold was discovered on the Rand. The President of the Transvaal Republic, Kruger, was happy to tax the goldminers heavily and to reserve all rights of citizenship for his own people. Rhodes, with the connivance of Joseph Chamberlain at the Colonial Office and Flora Shaw, the colonial editor of *The Times*, plotted a coup d'état in Johannesburg. The attempt failed; Dr Jameson, Cecil Rhodes's greatest friend, being captured by the Boers, and only released for trial in London after payment of a huge ransom. Kruger received an open telegram from the Kaiser, sent with the secret approval of the Imperial Government, congratulating him on his success over 'invading hordes'. Later Krupps sent out guns with which the Boers, crossing into Natal in 1899, bombarded Ladysmith. Natal was in great danger from this long-prepared attack, timed to coincide with the rains that made the veldt green for the invaders' horses. With better generalship the Boers could have swept their opponents into the sea. The British Army, however, was no longer the slow-moving gaily-coloured host of Crimean days. It had been entirely reorganised and under Roberts and Kitchener, generals already victorious in other campaigns, the colonies were saved. In England Liberals and Radicals expressed disgust at such imperialist aggression.

CHAPTER TWELVE

The Twentieth Century

The Monarchy

Victoria	1837–1901
Edward VII	1901–1910
George V	1910–1936
Edward VIII	1936
George VI	1936–1952
H.M. Queen Elizabeth II	1952–

The Royal Family and the Constitution

The funeral of Queen Victoria, attended by the crowned heads of Europe and their families, among whom her favourite grandson, the German Kaiser, was the most striking figure, caused all thoughtful men to ponder upon the mutability of states. The queen had been much more than a figurehead and had won the affection, as well as the respect, of the vast majority of her subjects. Men asked whether the monarchy, having reached such a peak from such a low trough in 1837, must inevitably wane during the coming century.

The cortège through the streets of London was a great military pageant carried out in time of war before immense crowds. The presence of so many soldiers and sailors was a reminder that the personal loyalty of every officer and man in the army and navy was in a special way directed towards the monarchy; they had volunteered in hundreds of thousands to serve the queen in South Africa; now their allegiance was to her eldest son.

Edward VII had reached his sixtieth year, and from youth had performed many tasks that his mother found distasteful. He had mixed with people of many different nations, travelling widely in order to acquaint himself with their beliefs and traditions, work and amusements. It was typical of him that on 14 February 1901 as the first act of his reign he opened Parliament in person, reviving a ceremony of great historic interest that had seldom been seen since the death of his father in 1861. The gorgeous robes, the splendour of the crown jewels, and the solemn assertion of the supreme power, not of Parliament but of the king in Parliament, struck deep into the subconscious minds of all present. Here the seeds were sown of certain unpredictable acts of political unselfishness which later saved the constitution and the country.

Of these occasions three are of special interest. When in 1910 the king died after a brief illness, the Conservative majority in the House of Lords was in the middle of a bitter struggle with the Liberal government. In order to allow the new king, George V, time to take stock of his position—he might have been asked to devalue the Upper House by immediately raising over a hundred members of the Liberal party to the peerage—both political parties agreed to set aside their strife for a period. At the end of this pause tempers had cooled and a compromise was reached.

In 1914, when Ireland was on the verge of civil war, and the Germans about to invade Belgium, the Irish nationalist leader, John Redmond, committed political suicide by announcing in the House of Commons that all the British troops stationed in Ireland to protect the Protestant minority might be withdrawn—the Irish would volunteer for the defence of the island.

On the third occasion George V's son, Edward VIII, whom many remembered as the boy who, first of all the subjects of the crown, had paid his father homage in Westminster Abbey, was advised, soon after his accession in 1936, that he must either abandon his plans to marry a twice-divorced American, or abdicate in favour of his brother. When he decided to abdicate, there were many who feared that the monarchy might not easily recover from his act, but so great was the affection with which the great-grandchildren of Victoria were regarded, and so multifarious the good and charitable works in which they, their wives and their families were engaged, that within a generation the reputation of the monarchy stood as high as it had ever done.

The advantages of living under a monarchy are not restricted to matters of patriotic feeling and historical association. A Head of State, whether king or president, is mortal, and must from time to time be replaced. Under republican constitutions a new contender for the supreme place must either advertise his own merits by standing for election or watch and wait while his qualifications are the subject of private discussion. Communist states either choose a nonentity or deify a celebrity. Only in a monarchy can the business of state continue without interruption, men of every shade of opinion having been mentally prepared in advance to accept their new ruler with loyal contentment.

The Rise of the Labour Party

During the nineteenth century the doctrines of socialism had been thoroughly discussed among intellectuals in every country of Europe and the most powerful version to emerge was that of Karl Marx (1818-1883). When he formed his dark and hostile view of the achievements of the industrial revolution he scarcely considered why it was that manual workers in Britain were rich compared with the agricultural populations of Asia and Africa. The ownership of the means of production, distribution and exchange was in private hands; there lay the evil; if it were transferred to 'the people', meaning the manual workers, all would be well; revolution and 'class war' were the means to attain this transfer. Religion, which had inspired most of the efforts of Parliament to protect women and children in industry and to better the conditions of the poorest paid workers, was 'the opium of the people'.

Russia was the first country to put Marxism into practice. Before the Russian

The House of Commons, destroyed by bombs, 10 May 1941. In this chamber, part of a large complex designed and built by Sir Charles Barry and Augustus Pugin between 1840 and 1857, the Speaker's chair was in the centre with the Government benches on his right and the Opposition on his left, as in the chapel of St Stephen previously used. There were not enough seats to accommodate all members simultaneously, but being a small chamber it favoured a persuasive conversational speaking style and swift interchange of question and answer. By Sir Winston Churchill's wish the new chamber built after the war was very similar to the old

revolutions of 1917 few people in Britain openly adopted Marxist doctrines. The leading Socialist writers, Bernard Shaw and H. G. Wells, knew too much from personal experience of the life of the poor to imagine that preaching revolution was the way to power; they belonged to the Fabian Society, which, as its name indicated, believed in gradualism. Others advocated co-operation with the Radicals in the Liberal party, and yet another group had formed an Independent Labour Party (ILP). Amid all these cross currents a big conference of Socialists and trade unionists was held in London in 1900 and Keir Hardie (1856-1915) of the ILP, who had been a member of Parliament from 1892 to 1895, proposed the formation of a Labour Representation Committee (LRC) which should organise the candidature of socialists in Parliamentary elections and form a group in the House with its own whips. Ramsay MacDonald (1826-1937) was this Committee's first secretary and the unions agreed to subscribe ten shillings per annum for every thousand members.

In the general election of 1900 a Tory government was returned with Arthur Balfour

(1848-1930) as Prime Minister. Two LRC men were elected, Keir Hardie and Richard Bell, of the Amalgamated Society of Railway Servants, later the National Union of Railwaymen, who was at this time involved in a dispute that had occurred on the Taff Vale Railway in South Wales. Against Bell's advice, the men had struck. The employers sued the union for damages and were awarded £32,000, a decision by Mr Justice Farwell which was quashed in the Appeal Court and upheld in the House of Lords. The unions had for thirty years assumed that they were immune from action for damages. Because no case had previously been brought against them, no distinction had been drawn between the right to withdraw labour, which in a free country none would deny, and 'the right to strike', which, by established convention, implied that those employed by a company before a dispute were entitled to have their jobs back when it was over. Nothing roused unions to greater fury than the appearance of blacklegs going in to do the work of those on strike. The unions therefore demanded, besides immunity from action for damages, the legal right to picket places of work during strikes. Such rights were so difficult for lawyers to define and police to enforce that Balfour set up a commission to explore the whole complex of trade union law. Before action could be taken on its findings, the Cabinet was split by a quarrel between the advocates of Free Trade and Imperial Preference and in 1905 Balfour resigned.

A general election followed in which Liberals won 377 seats, a majority of 84 over all other parties combined; the various Conservative groups had 157 seats, the Irish Nationalists 83 and Labour 53, of whom 29 had been sponsored by the LRC and the rest mainly by miners' unions. The Liberals at once passed a Trade Disputes Act which ignored the findings of the previous Government, exempted the unions from actions for damage and gave them a vaguely defined right to picket.

At this point the LRC renamed itself the Labour Party, but kept itself distinct both from the Parliamentary Party and from trade unions. Its speakers often referred to the Labour 'movement' in order to avoid the vulgar connotations of the word 'party', which might seem to put them on the same level as other politicians. In 1909 the party received a fresh blow from Mr Justice Farwell. The Walthamstow branch of the union that had fought the Taff Vale case brought, through its secretary, W. V. Osborne, a suit asking that contributions to the party from union funds should be declared illegal. Osborne won and the decision was upheld by all three judges in the Appeal Court and all five judges in the House of Lords. The union expelled Osborne and one of his friends, confiscating their contributions and terminating their benefits. The judges were perhaps right to decide that a union was not in the same category as a friendly society. Some Labour members of Parliament found their salaries stopped as a result of the Osborne decision, but in 1911 the Liberal government, headed by Herbert Asquith (1852-1928), instituted payment for members, and in 1913, following a great wave of strikes, passed a Trade Union Amendment Act under which money for political work could not be paid from general funds, but had to be raised through a separate political levy, from which non-Socialist members could 'contract out'. This had the opposite effect to the one Parliament intended; the income of the party was multiplied by ten; guaranteed regular amounts were available in the political fund of every affiliated union.

Between 1910 and 1914 the Labour party's reputation was badly damaged by the unions' failure to deal with a series of unofficial stoppages on the railways and in the mines, docks and textile industries. The big unions, even with their increased income, were financially weak, and never employed more than a handful of secretaries, all of them overworked and underpaid. Consequently they were unaware of what grievances were festering in distant parts of the country. To make matters worse there was a strange spirit of violence abroad among the whole population, exemplified by the arson and bomb outrages of the suffragettes and gun-running in Ireland, where Ulstermen feared Home Rule and prepared to fight against it. In a wave of strikes the picketing was far from peaceful. Miners in Tonypandy attacked the ventilating machinery at a pithead and a riotous mob looted and terrorised the whole neighbourhood. Troops had to be sent to help the police restore order. Serious plans were laid for a 'Triple Alliance' of miners, railwaymen and dockers in the belief that concerted action could so disrupt the economic life of the country that the government would be forced to hand over control to them. In France this policy was seen as a means of preventing troop movements if war should be declared, but when war came no union took action. Ramsay MacDonald resigned the leadership of the Labour Party, being a pacifist, and was not re-elected until 1922. Keir Hardie, also a pacifist, appealed to the miners of South Wales to strike against the war effort, but they would not listen and he died of a broken heart. To stop the war revolutionary forces far greater than the Labour movement were required. Within four years four great empires were reduced to ruins, those of Russia, Austria, Germany and Turkey.

The Great War, 1914-1918

War, as Karl von Clausewitz (1780-1831), the Director of the War Academy in Berlin, had said, and every German staff officer had learnt, is 'the continuation of policy'. The Kaiser's government had carefully planned to be ready for war in 1914 and to seek a pretext for it. British statesmanship could do nothing to prevent this. The Germans' goal was the domination of the land mass of Europe and Asia; they already had colonies in Africa and the Pacific; the future lay with the nation that could command a major oilfield, and they aimed at wells in Iraq, Persia and southern Russia. By allying themselves with the Austro-Hungarian Empire in its quarrels with the Serbs and other nations to the east, the Germans believed that they could halt the Russian advance to the Mediterranean and, with the Turks as their allies, extend the railway eastwards from Constantinople to the Mosul oilfield and on to Baghdad, south Persia and even Karachi; the British, beaten in Europe, would be unable to defend India.

Unfortunately for the Germans the two dominant races in the Austro-Hungarian empire were threatened by revolution before the war began. To appease their subject nationalities they had set up two parliaments based on manhood suffrage, one in Vienna in 1909 and one in Budapest in 1911. Debates had frequently ended in pandemonium, Czechs, Slovaks, Ruthenians, Croats and other minority groups competing in mutual recrimination. There was a risk that the conscripts sent by these minorities to the imperial army would turn their arms upon the Dual Monarchy, not upon its enemies. When on

28 June 1914 a member of the Austrian royal family, the Archduke Ferdinand, was shot dead in the streets of Sarajevo by Serbian conspirators, the imperial government decided to invade Serbia. The Archduke had not been popular either in Vienna or in Budapest, but it was considered, since revolution was being aided by states outside the empire, that war was the only solution.

To help the Serbs the Russians began mobilising their huge army. According to plan, the Germans also mobilised, and so did the French. General war resulted, with the Turkish empire joining the Central Powers. Britain entered the conflict on 4 August, having waited for the Germans to cross the neutral territory of Belgium in order to attack France from the north as well as the east. The Committee of Imperial Defence, set up in London under the Balfour government, had long been at work preparing a War Book with precise plans for moving a force of 100,000 men to France in ten days. The navy had already been mobilised, thanks to the initiative of the First Lord of the Admiralty, Winston Churchill, and the German navy made no attempt to disrupt the Channel passage, possibly because the British Expeditionary Force was regarded as contemptibly small. It was the best-trained and best-equipped army ever to leave the island, but its destination was vague. The commander-in-chief, Sir John French, having received little guidance and no help from the commander of the French left wing, advanced as far as Mons, where two British divisions went into action against odds of

Avro 504. A. V. Roe, afterwards Sir Alliot Verdon Roe, began building aircraft of this type in 1913. In 1909 he became the first to fly a heavier-than-air machine in Britain, and as a designer-constructor-pilot the first to fly a British-designed aircraft with a British engine. This was the fourth in his series of designs, but he numbered them from 500 to boost the prestige of his firm. The 504 was in service with the RFC in 1914 and was used to raid the Zeppelin sheds at Friederichshafen, the first organised bombing raid in history

three to one. A new service, the Royal Flying Corps, reported that a whole German army was moving south past the British left wing. Sir John ordered a retreat; his men covered 200 miles in thirteen days, carried through the scorching heat of each long mile by unforgettable marching songs and the pipes, fifes and drums of regimental bands. At the end of the retreat they turned to fight again. The allies, driven back almost to Paris, repulsed the Germans at the battle of the Marne early in September. In a swiftly moving campaign Sir John maintained a constant threat against the right wing of the enemy, who began to dig trenches and protect them with barbed wire, as the Boers had done. The British losses mounted; when winter came, hundreds of young officers had died, leading their men forward, sword in hand, against machine-guns; and half the British Expeditionary Force had been killed or wounded. To reinforce the line volunteers not only from Britain but from Canada, Australia, New Zealand, South Africa, and other parts of the Empire were posted to France. By the spring of 1915 over half a million British troops were engaged. The military deadlock on the western front was described to the Cabinet in London by Mr Winston Churchill early in 1915. Before the war he had either taken part in or reported wars in India, Egypt, Cuba and South Africa and now asserted with forceful prescience that, until the Allies had invented some kind of land battleship to get through wire and across trenches under fire, any further offensive in France should be postponed; but the slaughter went on.

To divert the enemy Churchill initiated an attack on the Dardanelles. In 1915 a force of British, Australian and New Zealand troops nearly succeeded in breaking through to Constantinople. If their commanders had acted with energy and drive, they would have opened up a route by which help would have been sent to the Russians, but the advantage of surprise was lost. The Turks under a German general forced the British to withdraw. In London this fresh defeat led to the fall of the Liberal government. The Prime Minister, Herbert Asquith, formed a coalition cabinet, leaving out Winston Churchill, who for a time went to fight in France. The new government was as inadequate as its predecessor, and at the end of 1916 a coalition of Liberals and Conservatives with one Labour minister, Arthur Henderson, was formed under the leadership of Lloyd George. Defeat had also caused the recall of Sir John French and the appointment of Sir Douglas Haig.

In Berlin deadlock in the west had set up similar tension. At the outset the Russians had invaded East Prussia, and a former commander-in-chief, Hindenburg, who had been called from retirement to conduct the campaign, repulsed the enemy with heavy loss. The church bells rang out to celebrate this victory at the moment when Moltke, the commander of all the German armies, was losing the battle of the Marne, a defeat which led to his recall. Hindenburg and Ludendorff, his chief of staff, expected to be given the supreme command at once. They had to wait a long time, for in the struggle at headquarters between the 'easterners' and 'westerners' hope of a breakthrough in France was not abandoned until after Pétain's successful defence of Verdun in 1916. On appointment Hindenburg received advice from his navy chiefs that gave him a good reason for being an 'easterner'. After the battle of Jutland in May 1916, at which each fleet had inflicted heavy loss on the other, the Germans had returned to port. They had no wish for another surface engagement but asserted that by unrestricted submarine warfare they could cause the British such severe losses of food imports that surrender would follow. Hindenburg accepted this proposal, since it left him free to retire to a strong defence line in the west and wait on events, while he attacked the remnants of the Russian army. In February 1917 Petrograd was paralysed by a general strike followed by sporadic but widespread army mutinies. Suddenly there was no will to fight or to work. The Tsar abdicated, and in the spring sunshine there were endless demonstrations, speeches and strikes.

In Britain the submarine blockade reduced food reserves to six weeks' supply. Then Lloyd George forced the Admiralty to adopt a convoy system, escorting merchant ships in large groups and using new inventions for tracking and depth charges for attacking submarines. Shipping losses were dramatically reduced. In London food rationing was not the only civilian hardship. There were frequent air raids, first from airships and then from aeroplanes. The loss of life was not great but the sight of searchlights and shell bursts and the noise of guns and aircraft engines were all novel and terrifying.

The Germans had hoped that shipping losses would not bring the United States into the war in time to save the Allies, but their calculations were upset by the British intelligence service, which passed to the Americans an intercepted German cable to the Mexican government offering armed help in their war against the United States. This enabled the President, Woodrow Wilson, to bring his country into the war in Europe. He had been re-elected in November 1916 by a very narrow majority, having stood out for neutrality. His declaration of war was accompanied by a statement welcoming the news of the Tsar's abdication. Not until a year later, when the Allies were near defeat in France, did the first two American divisions go into the line. Hindenburg had brought forty from Russia. Two Russian exiles also welcomed the news from Petrograd, a Jew in New York named Trotsky and Lenin in Switzerland. By a coup d'état in November 1917 they put an end to Wilson's vision of a new democratic republic.

In the east the year 1917 brought the first British land victories, won against the sprawling Turkish empire. Among the Arab subjects of the Turks in Arabia, Palestine and Syria the British fomented rebellion through agents such as Colonel T. E. Lawrence. In Mesopotamia Sir Stanley Maude, advancing up the Tigris with help from the Royal Navy, captured Baghdad in March 1917. He died of cholera soon afterwards, but his army eventually captured the Mosul oilfield. At the end of the year Sir Edmund Allenby, at the head of troops that had been stationed in Egypt to protect the Suez Canal, crossed the Sinai desert and captured Jerusalem, a holy city in the eyes of Moslems, Christians and Jews. On a pre-war visit there the Kaiser, dressed in a splendid uniform, had ridden in on a white horse; Allenby entered on foot with a few companions. The British Foreign Secretary, Arthur Balfour, impressed by the doctrine of Zionism, offered Palestine to the Jewish communities all over the world as 'a national home', a vague declaration from which the British reaped little gratitude and much trouble. In a further campaign ten months later Allenby drove the Turks out of Syria and captured Damascus. This ancient caravan capital should have been made the centre of an Arab empire, but at the

Paris peace conference the French demanded Syria as a reward of victory, and suppressed the Arabs by force.

The year 1917 was one of disaster in France and Italy. General Nivelle's army mutinied in May after a terrible defeat, and in July Haig started a great offensive in Flanders. The losses on the first day were 60,000, and mounted each week as ceaseless and unseasonable deluges of rain converted the shelltorn battlefield into an impassable quagmire. At Passchendaele the attack foundered with British losses of 244,000. Scarcely a village in England was without its mourners. The battle was hardly over before the Italians, who had been bribed to enter the war on the Allied side in 1915 by the promise of Austrian territory on their north-eastern frontier, were routed at Caporetto. They fled towards Venice and only the hurried dispatch of British and French troops from the western front enabled them to re-establish a line. The end of the war, which the people of both sides longed for, seemed very far away.

In March 1918 Ludendorff was ready for a final effort in Flanders. He forbade an artillery barrage and silently, in thick mist, a large section of the British front line was overrun. Behind it the enemy faltered, finding huge stores of food, though they had been told that Britain was starving. Their offensive was contained, and in August Haig counter-attacked; the infantry were protected by 400 long-awaited land-battleships (their manufacture had been concealed under the cover-name 'tank'). For the first time the German line broke. By September there was talk of an armistice, but the fighting

A Field Gun of the Royal Artillery stuck in Flanders mud near Zillebeke, 9 August 1917

Mark V Tanks going into action in August 1918. The infantry are New Zealanders

went on. The gigantic German war machine had no brakes; it ran on an iron chain of command and obedience; not until the Kaiser abdicated and was granted asylum in the Netherlands was it possible to blow the bugles for cease-fire. In Kiel the navy had already mutinied; and in Berlin the socialist members of the Reichstag had set up a republic. Hindenburg never admitted that the Allies had beaten him in battle; he 'brought the army home'. While he did so, a Bavarian lance-corporal was lying in hospital having been gassed at the front. The legend grew that the soldiers had been 'stabbed in the back' by socialists and Jews. The lance-corporal, whose name was Hitler, recovered and built up this story in a ceaseless flow of public oratory.

Propaganda of another sort had gained credence in Britain. President Wilson was given an ecstatic welcome in London; he had promised to go to the Paris peace conference and by 'open diplomacy' redraw the map of Europe only after ascertaining by plebescite the wishes of its various peoples; in future, international disputes would be settled by a new organisation, the League of Nations. To very few did a just peace ever come.

Pre-war Scientists: Post-war Achievements

During the Great War a Scottish doctor, Alexander Fleming (1881-1955), horrified by the damage done to the tissues of open wounds by attempting to disinfect them with iodine (a universal practice), began research at St Mary's Hospital, London, for a better method. In 1928 he made a report on penicillin mould which led in 1939 to the discovery by Dr Florey and Dr Chain of a process for making penicillin chemically, an invaluable invention that has probably saved more human lives than any other.

In nuclear physics the discoveries of J. J. Thomson at Cambridge in the 1890s and of his pupil Ernest Rutherford (1871-1937) gave Britain pre-eminence in twentieth century science. At Oxford Henry Moseley (1887-1915), who died in the Dardanelles campaign, invented an apparatus to establish atomic numbers and of this Rutherford wrote: 'The law of Moseley ranks in importance with the discovery of the periodic law of the elements and of spectral analysis and is in some ways more fundamental than either.' In 1919 Rutherford observed the splitting of the atom at the Cavendish Laboratory. This, like the discovery of penicillin, had at first no practical application but in conjunction with refugees, Albert Einstein (1879-1955) from Berlin and others from the university of Gottingen in Hanover, it was applied to the making of bombs and to the provision of nuclear power. British universities benefited greatly from the influx in the 1930s of German scholars expelled by Hitler. Einstein stayed at Oxford on his way to America and lectured at Rhodes House.

Great excitement was caused in 1901 when Marconi (1874-1937) achieved his first transatlantic radio transmission from Cornwall. He had come to Britain from Italy and received valuable help from William Preece, the chief engineer of the Post Office, and from Ambrose Fleming (1849-1945), who invented the thermionic valve in 1904. In

Fleming's diode, or 'oscillation valve', 1904. It could convert radio waves into pulses of direct current audible through a telephone receiver. In 1907 Lee de Forest invented the triode, enabling the valve to amplify and to generate high frequency oscillations. Without this sound broadcasting and television would have been impossible

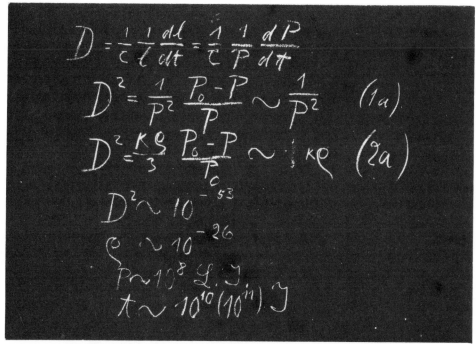

Formulae chalked by Albert Einstein on a blackboard he used when lecturing at Rhodes House, Oxford on 16 May 1931. His theory of relativity revolutionised mathematics

1928 the first transatlantic television transmission was made by John Logie Baird (1888-1946).

Under the stimulus of radio experiments great advances were also made in astronomy, for it was soon discovered that transmissions were affected by the change from night to day and by the incidence of sun spots. By the 1950s Britain had two excellent radio telescopes and began pioneer studies on many varied signals from outer space. No branch of science remained unaffected by the explosion of intellectual energy which occurred at the beginning of the century.

Willingly to School

In the election held immediately after the 1918 armistice Lloyd George spoke in his fervent way of 'a fit country for heroes to live in'. This never materialised, but in education his idealism bore fruit. He had appointed an Oxford don, H. A. L. Fisher, to plan a fresh advance in public education, and this was greeted by men of all parties as right and necessary. The 1918 Fisher Act 'raised the school-leaving age to fourteen', that is, it became illegal for parents to send a child out to work before its fourteenth birthday; no school fees were required, but parents were obliged to provide food, clothes and shelter, which sometimes proved difficult in poor families with many children. At the same time education committees of the various county and borough councils were legally obliged to build more classrooms and increase the number of teachers, the cost being highest in low-income areas with dense populations. Raising the school-leaving age was regarded by most educationists as a sign of grace in a government because it set up a goal for administrators to aim at, but few were able to predict costs or face the political consequences of imposing enough in taxation to fulfil their own promises. For example, Fisher, as President of the Board of Education, the department responsible for teaching of every kind, decided to raise the status of teachers by increasing their salaries and grading them on a national scale. He estimated that this would increase the cost by £3,000,000, but in the event it was ten times as much. Nor were the salaries paid from a central fund. Teachers lacked the prestige and promotion prospects enjoyed by civil servants.

The benefits of the Fisher Act were further spoiled by the sharp cleavage between the elementary and the secondary schools and their staffs. This arose from the historical circumstance that compulsory 'free' elementary education for all had been the object of the 1870 Act, though not achieved until the 1890s and even then not wholly free. The political parties had been driven reluctantly to create a department concerned only with the education of the poor, and intent on winning a battle against illiteracy, unemployment and crime in big cities. This battlefield had been taken over in the twentieth century by the new county and borough councils. The schools were half-financed from the rates and half by the central government with all the inherent defects that divided responsibility causes. The secondary schools were much newer institutions, many of them created as a result of the Balfour Education Act of 1902. Some of the old endowed grammar schools for boys and the Victorian foundations for girls received State grants and other help from local education authorities, which paid the fees of about one-third of the pupils in many schools. The staffs of the secondary schools were mainly recruited from university graduates, but these were given no test of their ability to maintain discipline in class and to transmit knowledge. They were paid much higher salaries than non-graduates serving on the same staff, and were pressed by the education authorities to submit their pupils at the end of a four-year course to one of the many examinations set by external boards at the universities. School inspectors and educationists observed disapprovingly that there was undue emphasis on preparation for these tests, but ambition spurred on pupils, teachers and parents, and employers soon began to insist on more and better qualifications.

In the elementary schools a minority of the staffs were graduates, a majority men and women who had passed through teachers' training colleges, and a minority who had no special qualifications other than a desire to teach and skill in handling large classes. They were faced with the legal obligation to follow a syllabus in their senior classes for pupils of eleven to fourteen years of age similar to that provided for their cleverer brothers and sisters who had passed into grammar schools. Only a few ever obtained school-leaving certificates of the kind obtained by secondary school pupils. From the age of eleven such pupils often suffered from a sense of failure, lacked the will to work and longed for the day when they could leave school and earn wages. Bitterness grew in the classrooms and on the staffs.

The Second World War, like the First, created a ferment of ideas and an intense longing to create a better educational system. In 1943 a Conservative, R. A. (later Lord)

Butler, presented to Parliament a scheme for a tripartite system of secondary schools, at which the school-leaving age was to be fifteen, no fees were to be charged and there was to be a choice of three types of four-year course, grammar, modern and technical. The independent grammar schools and public schools were to be left untouched, though the public schools had faced a crescendo of criticism ever since 1918. Socialists inveighed against the 'divisive' privilege enjoyed by boys and girls whose parents paid the high fees they charged, yet their waiting lists grew longer and longer. The Labour Party, which came to power with a big majority in 1945, found that the war had created such severe shortages of teachers and buildings that even the comparatively small relief afforded by the independent schools was welcome. Their ancient statutes and endowments were left intact, only to come under fresh attack during the Labour Administration of 1964 to 1970. Once more they survived.

As a result of the Butler Act of 1944, a much vaguer and less effective law than at first planned, the elementary schools sent all their senior pupils at the age of eleven to some kind of secondary school. The selection examinations which they took were designed to discover what kind of education would suit the ability and aptitude of each child. They included intelligence tests said to be capable of eliminating any advantage gained by children from their social background. As in 1918, neither the teachers, buildings nor finance required by such ambitious legislation were forthcoming. Soon Socialists were complaining that the selection examinations were unfair. Cramming for them became widespread. By 1970 pressure from all sides on the local education authorities had caused them to terminate the tests in most areas. In some places new comprehensive schools for 1,500 to 2,000 pupils were built, providing a wider choice of subjects.

The great gain within the classrooms from over half a century of reform came not from any administrative jugglery but from the slow permeation throughout society of a more kindly and understanding spirit. This enabled many different reforms to become effective. In schools of every type it brought about a new informality and friendship between teachers and taught. A good education became universally acknowledged as something deeper and more lasting than the acquiring of this or that snippet of knowledge about literature or science. It was seen as a process continuing from the cradle to the grave and even beyond it, for the ancient Greek philosopher Plato, the Talmud and the Fathers of the Christian Church had all taught that man was no mere finite creature of the visible world, but had within him intimations of immortality.

The Second World War: 1939–1945

That Britain should have been obliged, much against her will, to go to war with Germany in 1939 after utterly defeating her in 1918 seems inexplicable by any ordinary historical analysis. That the Germans should have deliberately provoked a second conflict, and persisted in it until their country was partitioned, is proof that men live more by dreams than reason.

The British dream, powerfully stimulated by the Liberal idealism of President Wilson at the Paris peace conference in 1919, was of a world in which any two nations in dispute would, rather than risk another holocaust such as that of 1914, submit their quarrel to an international council for settlement and abide by its judgement. Such was the assumption behind the Covenant of the League of Nations, and even after Wilson, smitten by a fatal paralysis, had failed to persuade the United States Congress to accept either the Covenant or the peace terms, the British people clung to this visionary scheme. As late as 1935 they sent to Parliament an elaborate petition containing over 11,500,000 signatures in favour of disarmament and 'collective security'.

The mirage pursued by the French was of a different kind. They were not interested in the League of Nations except as a means of additional security. Grief for their war dead, and anger over the hundreds of town and villages reduced to rubble in the fighting, ruled their hearts. The German homeland suffered no such destruction. Clemenceau, who had seen the Prussian invasion of France in 1870, an ideal representative for his country, insisted on a hard peace and a huge indemnity, sufficient to pay for the reconstruction of homes, farms and factories. Nearly five years after the armistice the French army of occupation in the Rhineland marched into the rich industrial area of the Ruhr, intent on collecting the war indemnity. There the workers met them with passive resistance, and the bankers attempted an arranged devaluation of the currency. This became uncontrolled and the mark worthless, a disaster which caused vast damage and suffering, but effectively cheated the French, who withdrew to the zone of occupation. In fear of German revenge, they then built a costly system of underground fortresses on their eastern frontier, called the Maginot line, but it was never finished and did not protect northern France.

It would still have been possible to enforce the Versailles treaty if the Allied occupation forces, which remained in Germany until 1929, had been used by their governments as something more than showpieces. Instead, the German people were allowed to live on memories. They laid the blame for their sufferings on this minority and on that, but never on the army, the historical foundation of their lost greatness. According to legend, the great medieval emperor, Frederick Barbarossa, founder of the First Reich, was not dead but sleeping; and the Second Reich was not forgotten. The survivors from the Kaiser's army, navy and air force were beginning to discuss how the errors of 1914 could be rectified, next time, when suddenly in their midst was a young soldier called Hitler, small and pale, but possessed of demonic energy, bewitching audiences of every kind with his talk of a Third Reich, of a broken Germany that would rise again. To millions of ordinary citizens everything he did and said seemed to bring the millenium a step nearer. The hunger and inflation of the 1920s, the unemployment, the widows who still wept, the shell-shocked and limbless silent in their chairs no longer mattered. Through the clean towns, along the mountain roads and into the trim forests men marched again and sang, holding high banners and torches, listening to the vague, hot, menacing promise that they would be a Herrenvolk once more.

In 1932, just ten years after Mussolini and the Fascist party had seized power in Rome, Hitler was appointed Chancellor of Germany. His National Socialist Party (Nazis) was the biggest single party but did not have an absolute majority. Early in 1933 he eliminated the eighty Communist deputies in the Reichstag and his dictatorship began. Between

1936 and 1939 German airmen were sent to co-operate with General Franco's forces in the Spanish civil war. Their exploits against defenceless Basques frightened all Europe. Franco received even more aid in soldiers and tanks from Italy, where Mussolini had just succeeded in his defiance of the sanctions imposed by the League of Nations, and annexed Abyssinia.

Austria was overrun by the Germans in the spring of 1938. This left the frontiers of Czechoslovakia vulnerable on three sides. They had been drawn to include a large German minority which, Hitler pretended, was being oppressed. The French and British, though bound by treaty to defend the Czechs, were anxious to avoid war. The British armed forces were short of both men and machines, and the Prime Minister, Neville Chamberlain, went to meet Hitler in Munich, where it was agreed that the Czechs should be compelled to surrender the German-speaking areas and their frontier defences. Chamberlain, who had succeeded his closest friend, Stanley Baldwin, in 1937, returned from Germany to find himself immensely popular with all parties. Within a year Hitler had incorporated the Czechs in the Reich and attacked Poland, another country which Britain had promised to protect. The British and French declared war, but did not attack western Germany. The Germans, allied with the Russians, crushed the Polish army and partitioned the country. After this coup, delivered without warning, Hitler felt free to attack in the west, especially as the Russian army demonstrated its inefficiency in a winter war with Finland.

In the spring of 1940 Hitler ordered the invasion of three neutral countries, Denmark, Norway and the Netherlands. British navy and army units attacked the Germans in Norway but were forced to withdraw. This defeat brought a revolt in the Conservative party against Chamberlain, who resigned and shortly afterwards died of cancer. Winston Churchill, who had given many unheeded warnings of the German menace in the 1930s, became Prime Minister. Knowing that the Labour party, which had refused to join Chamberlain's government, would serve under him, he declared on 13 May: '*I have nothing to offer but blood, toil, tears and sweat. You ask, What is our policy? I will say: It is to wage war by sea, land, and air, with all our might and with all the strength that God can give us. You ask, What is our aim? I can answer in one word: Victory—victory at all costs, victory in spite of all terror; victory, however long and hard the road may be.*' The British dream had ended, and Hitler had no conception what mental and moral forces he had unleashed. The very thought that the whole business must be done again gave energy to every man, to the Prime Minister most of all. The idea of defeat was rejected. In some families father, mother, sons and daughters were all in uniform.

Two days after Churchill's appointment the Dutch army capitulated, and the Queen of the Netherlands followed the King of Norway to Britain, where both set up governments in exile. The ten British divisions on the continent left the positions which they had prepared during the winter and advanced to meet the enemy, who were about to invade France with 134 divisions. Soon the British had been split off from the main strength of the French and, to save them, their commander, Lord Gort, ordered a fighting withdrawal to the coast at Dunkirk. From there 860 small ships from England ferried them back from the port and the beaches; operating with some cover from the Royal

Air Force, they rescued 338,226 men of whom 139,097 were French. It was a great deliverance.

In July 1940 the Luftwaffe, in preparation for the invasion of England, began bombing fighter stations in Kent and Surrey, while the Royal Air Force raided the concentrations of barges on the French coast. A large part-time volunteer force, the Home Guard, mustered to deal with possible parachute attacks of the kind used against the Dutch. Fighter Command found that its twenty radar stations of a type invented in 1935 by Sir Robert Watson Watt gave enough warning of the direction, altitude and number of approaching enemy bombers for squadrons ready on the ground to be ordered up for interception and guided into battle by ground-to-air radio. This 'battle of Britain' lasted until September. Against the Germans, who expected easy victory, the high morale of their opponents was decisive, more sorties being flown each day than seemed possible if the physical strain alone is considered. Not a single man from the commander-in-chief, Sir Hugh Dowding, to the newest mechanic had ever fought a battle like this before. The British pilots were reinforced by men from Poland, Czechoslovakia and the Commonwealth and their resistance changed the course of world history. On 17 September, Hitler, after losing sixty aircraft in a single day's fighting, gave orders postponing the invasion. Like Napoleon in 1805 he turned to the east, and began planning the invasion of Russia. The Luftwaffe remained, raiding Coventry, London, Birmingham and other towns at night throughout the winter and spring. The heart of

Vapour Trails over St Paul's Cathedral, London, 1940. During the Battle of Britain German bombers attacking London had fighter escorts who were engaged at great heights by RAF Spitfires and Hurricanes. Fighters sometimes left these vapour trails in the upper air

the city of London was destroyed by fire bombs and the chamber of the House of Commons was gutted. Anti-aircraft guns and night-fighters could do little damage to the enemy. On the ground fire, civil defence and nursing services were all improvised to deal with the Blitz, as it was called. In the long, slow watches they kept, interspersed with days and nights of horror and exhaustion, men and women showed exemplary patience and fortitude. These costly services remained on duty until the end of the fighting in Europe because the government knew, but could not reveal, German plans for sending over pilotless jet aircraft and rockets, both carrying heavy high-explosive charges, against which there was no known means of defence. In southern England these weapons, called V1 and V2, caused vast damage and much loss of life in the spring and summer of 1944, especially in the London area, where the war total of homes destroyed exceeded that in all other parts of the kingdom put together.

Mussolini had refrained from declaring war until after the fall of France. At once his 'Roman Empire' in Africa was in danger and in the first days of 1941 a small armed force stationed on the western border of Egypt, one of many in the Middle East under General Wavell's command, cut the communications of an Italian army of 300,000 in Cyrenaica; 113,000 Italians surrendered, and 1,300 guns were captured. The British lost 438 killed, most of them Australians. This victory, having regard to the smallness of Wavell's means and the magnitude of the result, was the most notable in the whole war. Unfortunately it provoked Hitler into sending out a corps under Rommel equipped with far better tanks than the British and he soon recaptured Cyrenaica except Tobruk. Technical superiority in tank-building remained with the Germans throughout the war.

The government in London next ordered Wavell to send forces to the aid of Greece, since the Germans, having overrun Jugoslavia, were pressing southward. Many were lost at sea and on land in this hopeless campaign, but, by delaying the invasion of Russia for a few weeks, it may have entangled the Germans for the first time in Russian mud, frost and snow. They were brought to a halt just outside Moscow.

The 'battle of the Atlantic' against German submarines and fast, heavily armed battleships and battle cruisers that could sink most of the ships in any convoy they intercepted was a long struggle with many vicissitudes and seemingly endless loss of life. The Irish government, though it allowed men to volunteer for service with the British, would not allow Irish bases to be used for aircraft and surface vessels. Tens of thousands of merchant seamen were drowned because of this interdiction, which left them a gap to cross in mid-Atlantic without escort. Not until 1943, when the Americans provided a large number of destroyers, and the Portuguese allowed aircraft bases in the Azores, did the Germans lose so many crews and U-boats that replacements could not be found.

Virtually unsinkable ships like the *Bismarck*, *Tirpitz*, *Scharnhorst* and *Gneisenau* gave the Royal Navy constant concern and many lives were lost in attempts to destroy them. In 1941 *Bismarck*, in her first engagement, hit *HMS Hood*, which blew up, and damaged *HMS Prince of Wales*; then, shadowed by a British flying-boat, she was intercepted and sunk, fighting against heavy odds. *Tirpitz* was sunk in a Norwegian fiord by British midget submarines in 1943.

At the end of 1941 the destruction by the Japanese of the United States fleet as it lay moored in Pearl Harbour, an attack delivered from aircraft carriers without declaration of war, caused an explosion of anger throughout America and the whole country mobilised with great speed for hostilities on two fronts. In China, where the Japanese had already been campaigning for four years, they could not overcome Chiang Kai-shek's forces in Chungking, but on the fall of France they had seized Vietnam and now quickly overran the Philippines, Hongkong, Malaya, Burma, the East Indies and many Pacific islands. For a time India was in danger, partly because the Indian nationalists refused to co-operate in their own defence, and partly because the British had few forces available to send out.

The progress of the Germans was first halted in the autumn of 1942. The lines of communication to their fighting men in North Africa and on the Volga were now dangerously long and vulnerable, and for the first time they met much superior forces. General Montgomery by his victory at Alamein removed the threat of invasion from Egypt and from Palestine. The Russians, by repulsing the Germans at Stalingrad, removed the danger that they would cross Asia and join forces with the Japanese.

British losses at Alamein were high, and Rommel, who extricated a large part of his force after the battle, was not expelled from Africa until the next year, when Montgomery's Eighth Army linked up with an Anglo-American force which had landed in Algeria. The British and Americans then fought their way ashore in Sicily, where the Germans had valuable airfields. This led to the deposition of Mussolini and peace negotiations with Marshal Badoglio. The British prisoners of war in Italy made the mistake of thinking that the Italians would send them home; instead they were rounded up by the Germans, who were only slowly and with great difficulty dislodged from the peninsula after nearly two years of bitter fighting.

The Allies now made plans for the liberation of France. In Britain whole counties assumed the appearance of armed camps as division after division arrived from America. The Russians, and many Communist sbop stewards and Left-wing journalists in Britain, caused much discontent in 1943, arguing that Churchill was delaying the opening of a Second Front because he did not wish to relieve the pressure on the Russian front. There were more strikes than at the worst period of the Great War, and the Government could make no effective reply, because it could not reveal the number of landing craft, floating jetties, pipeline and other devices that had to be manufactured and supplied with trained crews before a defended shore could be attacked. When the Russians refused to help the Polish Liberation Army in Warsaw, or to allow the Royal Air Force to do so, these critics remained silent.

As the larger part of the invasion forces were American, the supreme post was given to Eisenhower, and the command of the land forces to Montgomery. Victory in Normandy was won before the Germans could bring in reserves from the north. Paris was liberated and the Germans driven into the northern part of the Netherlands. A difference of opinion then arose at the Allied headquarters. Montgomery favoured advance on a narrow front through Holland into Germany. Eisenhower decided on a broad push eastward. In the Ardennes the Germans temporarily broke the American

Battalion Orders 25 November 1944. The Hampshires were the direct regimental descendants of Meredith's infantry who marched under Marlborough to the Danube in 1704

lines, and another winter of war ensued before the Rhine was crossed and the fighting spread into Germany. Hitler, almost forgotten, died in Berlin. Madness prevented him from ordering a cease-fire. The Russians, Americans and British soldiers met, and for a very short space, embraced.

The scenes of devastation and misery in Germany were the most appalling ever recorded. There were the mass graves at the concentration camps; the millions of foreigners released from German factories; 'displaced persons' in all directions seeking for food and shelter; the orphans of Jews, like the little girl who, asked her destination, said: 'I am going to Jerusalem'; the prisoners of war, of whom thousands had endured five years' confinement; and the vast heaps of rubble that had been fair cities before the Allied bombing began. This time there was no peace, only armistice. Churchill was 'dismissed' and Clement Attlee became Prime Minister, the first to have a large Labour majority. The partition of Germany by the Russians became permanent. Warsaw, Prague, Budapest, Bucharest, and Sofia were already in their hands.

Away in Burma the forgotten Army, the Fourteenth under General Slim, was engaged on the reconquest of a country still occupied by the Japanese, but two years later handed over to the Burmese administration. In the East Indies the Dutch remained deprived of an empire stretching over 3,000 miles. In Japan, a land where the military

169

tradition had always taught that death was preferable to surrender, the Emperor ordered a cease-fire on 14 August after atomic bombs had exploded over Hiroshima and Nagasaki.

The Enjoyment of Leisure

In the first part of the century the first objective for those under the necessity of earning a living was to acquire some leisure. Sunday was the only full day of rest in the week, a blessing for which the seventeenth century Puritans deserved, but seldom received, thanks. In England four Bank Holidays each year had been created by Parliament in Victoria's reign to compensate for some of the lost saints' days that Catholic countries still enjoyed, and they had become national festivals in which all delighted to take cheap train and boat excursions or charabanc rides into the country and down to the seaside, happy in spite of the fact that most employers, until 1947, stopped a day's wages for the holiday.

For women, opportunities to spend their leisure outside the home were rare. Apart from the textile trades of Yorkshire and Lancashire, there was little well-paid work for them, and for mothers of families shopping, cooking, cleaning, sewing and mending left little free time, yet, as in Victorian times, wives and mothers were not regarded as 'cabbages' if they remained at home and made that their pride and joy. In the evenings singing round the piano, reading stories, card-playing, magic lantern shows and puppet theatres were all popular ways of providing hospitality and entertainment. The habit of reading, which the Victorians regarded so highly, was learned in such households, and the public libraries which they founded became in the 1930s a splendid public service, carrying new books of every kind into the remotest country hamlets.

Talk of the emancipation of women, the constant theme of the law-abiding women suffragists, and the violent demonstrations of the suffragettes between 1906 and 1914, genuinely puzzled men, whatever their rank in society. The miners and dockers who voted for Ramsay MacDonald and Keir Hardie did not follow them in their support of Emmeline Pankhurst, who was both the suffragettes' leader and an ardent Socialist. Working men knew that when women got ideas into their heads somebody else did the washing up. Most kinds of public entertainment, especially horse-racing, cricket and football matches, catered mainly for men. Then, during the 1914-18 war, a new phenomenon, the cinema, began to flourish, delighting audiences of both sexes and all ages with the comedies of Charlie Chaplin and his rivals and endless dramas in American settings. Occasionally there was a horrifying newsreel from the western front. Talking pictures and colour followed in the 1930s, together with the mock grandeur and comfort of enormous picture palaces. The film industry achieved by the simple method of entertaining men and women together at very low prices a gradual reformation of manners; the noisy drunken roughness of Edwardian days was almost forgotten.

War service at home and abroad between 1914 and 1918 gave women a new prestige and money to spend, but little increase of leisure. After both the wars men returning to civilian life displaced the women who had been doing their work for a fraction of their pay, and only after 1945 did trade expand sufficiently to provide women in millions,

170

rather than thousands, with employment outside the home. Yet the new five-day week of forty-two hours, with extra pay for overtime, made little difference to them. The working woman returned in the evening, laden with the food that she had spent her lunch break buying, and it was she who was expected to do the cooking and provide company for sick or aged relatives, not her husband or brothers. 'Men must work and women must weep,' the old saying went. After emancipation women had to do both.

Few people fully enjoy their leisure hours in isolation, and the dwindling size of the farming population in the Highlands of Scotland, the mountains of Wales and the plains of England was due as much to the monotony of the long winter nights as to the neglect of agriculture by all governments. Popular education was also to blame; it was urban-based and puritanical in outlook, especially in Wales. There it had changed a happy, country population, lacking in political consciousness, into a people devoted to the hymns of William of Pantycelyn and to the Bible, which they knew both in the Welsh and English versions, and increasingly nationalistic in their politics. Hymn singing both in Wales and England became almost a substitute for religion. In schools of all kinds hymns were the central feature of every morning and evening assembly, and enjoyed by almost everyone, for the English, no less than the Welsh, are a singing nation. Music in Britain seemed to come out of the sky, the forests and the fields. Cecil Sharp, before mechanical recording was practicable, collected from many different counties folk tunes, dances and songs, listening to and writing down the various versions remembered by old people and saving them from the silence of antiquity. On a grander scale the Three Choirs Festival, held in turn in the medieval cathedrals of Worcester, Hereford and Gloucester, aroused in audiences a love of the past and of its music. It was no accident that three influential twentieth-century composers were born in that part of the world, Vaughan Williams and Gustav Holst in Gloucestershire and Elgar in Worcestershire. The Malvern hills and the Severn valley were clearly part of Elgar's inspiration. He once told an orchestra to play a passage in his first symphony 'like something we hear down by the river'. Similarly at a later date the Suffolk scene entered into the music of Benjamin Britten.

Gustav Holst, after playing the trombone in the Scottish Orchestra, settled in London, became director of music at St Paul's School for Girls, and developed many musical activities at Morley College. So successful was his teaching that music soon became part of the curriculum in many other schools, and formed a valuable corrective to the prevailing utilitarian outlook. Musicians, unlike other artists, produce nothing solid or permanent; however often they sing an aria or play a sonata, the music dies as soon as it is born; only the audience knows what it was like, a memory, perhaps of the sweetest, which none can divulge.

By a happy combination of circumstances the whole musical life of England was transformed between the wars by the British Broadcasting Corporation (BBC), a new semi-government, semi-private institution, to which Parliament gave a monopoly of radio and an assured income. In the early 1920s thousands listened with head phones on their ears plugged in to 'crystal' receivers, fed from high 'washing-line' aerials in the back garden. Everyone was supposed to pay a licence fee for each receiver. They heard only a pale, distorted image of the studio performance, but it sufficed; the fire was lit, and the fees poured in so quickly that the Post Office never troubled to collect from defaulters.

At the time the gramophone companies were selling hand-wound clockwork record players driving steel needles through the grooves of hard flat disks at 78 revolutions per minute. The young in most families soon wore them out with repeated encores; to them the gramophone was a ladder to heaven and the distortion did not matter. The manufacturers attacked the BBC monopoly but fortunately it had a Scottish engineer at the head of affairs, John Reith. He was 'a son of the manse', and later had a Latin version of St Paul's letter to the Philippians, chapter 4, verse 8, set in large bronze letters over the entrance to the studios in Broadcasting House; it was the theme of his long reign as Director-General. The right to broadcast recorded music was firmly upheld, and the minute sums worked out for 'needle time', soon amounting to millions of pounds, were paid to living composers and performers. With the engineering improvements and the free advertising provided by the BBC the gramophone companies expanded out of all recognition and the public concerts broadcast from London, Manchester and other centres won the admiration of every musician in the United Kingdom.

Speech naturally had to take second place to music as radio entertainment. Millions were delighted by the variety and abstruseness of the information which poured through the microphone, especially as better receivers made it possible to listen and do housework simultaneously Here was much that could never be learned from books, but came straight from the life experience of explorers, travellers, fishermen, naturalists, aviators, artists, craftsmen, collectors and many others. Yet few masters of the written word cared to write for radio; it seemed that the art of the spoken word was not worth learning. They did not reflect upon the broadcasting skill of Roosevelt, Churchill and de Gaulle.

The Second World War was not, like the First, followed by debilitating unemployment for millions. In a way that few could explain, and fewer still approved of, the rich nations grew richer. War service had split up families and mixed up the population to an unprecedented degree. On demobilisation southerners found themselves working in the north, country people came to town, and on a far bigger scale than before the war the urge to own a home of one's own, however high the mortgage, was actually fulfilled. Mechanical diggers and bulldozers enabled vast new suburbs to be built. For the inhabitants there was at first a lonely dullness in these places, a sense of being lost, when suddenly, after the Queen's coronation in 1953, everyone was talking about the BBC's television broadcast of the ceremony, how the cameras had taken viewers right to the very steps of the throne and introduced them in almost personal fashion to all the great people of the kingdom. Soon to possess a television set was the first priority even in the poorest homes. Now it was not a longed-for occasion to go out to the cinema; there was a home cinema for every night, a comfort for the lonely, the sad and the bored. The BBC's monopoly did not last very long.

Out of doors the new wealth also brought to millions ways of spending leisure that had previously been reserved for the rich. By the 1960s hundreds of thousands owned cars and boats; others took foreign holidays, travelling by air, and some joined clubs for motor racing, rock-climbing, gliding and flying. Yet perhaps the most universal pursuit remained that of gardening. In both wars people had taken allotments, 'dug for victory' and grown the family's potatoes and vegetables, but even then flowers were never neglected. In peace time cottage gardens, allotments by railway sidings, window boxes in cities, borders in suburban plots blossomed with a medley of pansies and pinks, roses and marigolds, lavender and lilac, Madonna lilies and Michaelmas daisies. To cultivate such beautiful things was seldom an act of conscious artistry, though it often enhanced, or redeemed, the surrounding architecture. The long hours spent on pruning and watering were reckoned pleasure, not work. Few gardeners, however learned about propagating roses or grafting fruit trees, regarded themselves as intellectuals, though the brain power they exercised put many bookworms to shame. They did not know that Shakespeare had named their flowers in his verses or that Constable had painted their countryside. When winter came and the flowers perished, none asked, Where is the profit? In a world increasingly insistent that everyone should be professional, they remained proudly amateur, and so in good company, for some of the greatest of their countrymen, past and present, were amateurs. King Alfred, a successful general, learnt to read and write; Sir Walter Raleigh, a literary man, became an explorer; Oliver Cromwell, a country gentleman, mastered statesmanship; and Sir Winston Churchill, a statesman, practised bricklaying. In this fashion each found harmony within himself. In a century of discord and violence, could leisure be better spent?

View from a cottage garden, Selworthy, Somerset

INDEX

Aberdeen University 69
Agincourt, battle of 67
Agriculture, Board of 124
Alamein, battle of 168
Alfred, King 23, 41, 172
Allenby, Sir Edmund 157
Amiens, peace of 133
Angles 17
Anglese 47
Anne, Queen 115, 129; Boleyn 81; of Cleves 84
Anti-Slavery Movement 131, 132, 136
Arabic numerals 36
Arbroath, Declaration of 53, 54
Architecture, Romanesque 33, 41, 60; Decorated 60; Perpendicular 60
Ark Royal 94
Armada, Spanish 94, 95
Arthur, King 17
Asquith, Herbert 153
Atlantic, battle of 167
Atomic bombs 170
Avro aircraft 155

Bacon, Roger 49
Baird, James Logie 161
Bakewell, Robert 123
Ball, John 57, 58
Ballot, secret 137
Balfour, Arthur 152, 153, 157
Bank of England 108, 113
Bannockburn, battle of 53
Baptists 105
Bayeux Tapestry 27, 28
Beaton, Cardinal 87
Beaufort, Lady Margaret 87
Becket, Thomas à 38, 39
Bede 17
Berkeley Castle 59
Bessemer, Sir Henry 145
Bible, translations of 63, 79, 80
Black Death 59
Black Prince 56, 57

Black Watch 119
Blenheim, battle of 115
Blitz 167
Boers 149
Bolingbroke, Henry 59
Boroughs, Rotten 136
Boston Stump 77
Bothwell, Earl of 91
Boulton, Matthew 126
Bourne, William 92
Boyle, Robert 113
Boyne, battle of 106
Breda, Declaration of 105
Bridgewater Canal 128
Brindley, James 128, 129
Britain, battle of 77, 166
Broadcasting, British Corporation 171
Bruce, King Robert 47, 52
Burma 168, 169
Butler, Lord 163

Cabot, John 73
Caesar, Julius 13, 14, 15
Canterbury Cathedral 38, 39, 57, 60
Canute, King 26
Caractacus 15
Caroline, Queen 120
Catherine of Aragon 81; Howard 84; Parr 84
Caxton, William 64, 72
Celts 13
Chamberlain, Neville 165
Chancellor, Richard 93
Charles I 99; II 103, 104, 105, 113
Chartists 138
Chaucer, Geoffrey 61, 62, 64
Children, employment of 142, 143
Chiswick House 122
Christianity, coming of 19
Chronicle, Anglo-Saxon 23, 28
Churchill, John Duke of Marlborough 115
Churchill, Sir Winston 149, 155, 156, 165, 172

Cistercians 40, 82
Clarkson, Thomas 132
Clerk-Maxwell, James 146
Coaches 128
Coke, Thomas 123
Commonwealth 104
Conservative Party 141
Cook, James 93
Coram, Thomas 129
County Councils 141, 162
Covenanters 103, 104
Cranmer, Archbishop 75, 81
Crécy, battle of 56
Crichton, Sir William 69
Crimean War 147
Cromwell, Oliver 103, 104, 105, 107, 172
Cromwell, Thomas 81, 82, 83
Crusades 33
Crush, William 146
Culloden, battle of 121
Czechs 154, 165, 168

Danegeld 22, 26, 28
Darby, Abraham 125
Darien 108
Darnley, Lord 91
Darwin, Charles 145
David I 34; II 54; of Wales 45
Disraeli, Benjamin 140, 148
Domesday Book 28, 30
Donald of the Isles 66
Douglas, Earls of 66, 69
Dowding, Sir Hugh 166
Drake, Sir Francis 93, 94, 95
Dunbar, battle of 104
Duncan I 26; II 25
Dundee, Viscount 106
Dunkirk 115, 165

Edgar, King of England 24
Edward I 45, 46, 52; II 52, 59; III 55; IV 72; V 72; VI 84, 86; VII 150; VIII 151; the Confessor 26, 49

174

Einstein, Albert 160
Eisenhower, General 168
Eleanor of Aquitaine 35
Elgar, Sir Edward 171
Elizabeth I 91; II 172; Woodville 72, 76; of York 73
Emancipation, Catholic 137; of Women 171
Enclosures 121, 124
English, language 41, 64
Erasmus 78, 79, 80
Ethelred the Unready 26
Eton College 73, 74
Euclid 36, 93

Fabian Society 152
Farwell, Justice 153
Fire of London 110
Fisher, H. A. L. 161, 162
Fisher, Bishop 82
Flanders mud 158
Fleming, Alexander 159
Fleming, Ambrose 160
Flodden, battle of 78
Foundling Hospital 129
Franklin, Benjamin 116, 117
French, Sir John 155
Friars 49

Gaelic 78
Gardeners 172
Gaunt, John of 57, 58
George I 118; II 116, 120; III 124; IV 133; V 61, 151; VI 150
George, Lloyd 156, 157
Georgia 130
Gibraltar 115
Gladstone, William 140, 148
Glasgow, Cathedral 88; University 69, 126
Glass, Stained 76
Glastonbury 24, 48
Glencoe 106
Glyn Dwr 65
Golden Hind 94
Grey, Earl 136; Sir George 147; Lady Jane 84
Gunpowder 68
Guns, naval 91
Guthrum, King 23

Hadrian's Wall 15
Haig, Sir Douglas 156, 158
Hamilton, Patrick 87
Hampshire Regiment 169
Hampton Court 80
Hardie, Keir 152, 170

Harding, Stephen 40
Harold I 25; II 26; Hardrada 26
Harvard, John 87
Harvey, William 112
Hastings, battle of 27
Henderson, Arthur 156
Henry I 33, 35; II 35; III 49; IV 65, 66; V 67; VI 67, 69, 72, 73, 74; VII 72; VIII 78, 80, 81, 82, 87, 92; Hotspur 66
Hindenburg 156, 159
Hitler 159, 164
Holy Island 20
Home Guard 166
Hospitallers, Knights 37
Howard, Lord Admiral 94
Hundred Years' War 55, 67, 68

Imperial Defence, Committee of 155
Intelligence Tests 163
Iona 20
Ireland, conquest begun 36
Irish Nationalists 153
Isabella, Queen 59

James I 68; II 69; III 65; IV 73, 78; V 87; VI and I 91, 99; II 105, 115
Jameson, Dr 149
Jane Seymour, Queen 84
Japan 67, 168, 169, 170
Joan of Arc 68
John, King 35, 42, 43, 44
Johnson, Dr Samuel 131
Jutes 17
Jutland, battle of 156

Kaiser, William II 149, 150
Kelvin, Lord 146
Killiecrankie, battle of 106
Kitchener, Lord 149
Knight, Joseph 131
Knox, John 88, 89, 90, 91

Labour Party, rise of 151, 152, 153
Lancaster, House of 69
Lancaster, James 95
Laud, Archbishop 101, 103
League of Nations 159, 164
Leslie, Alexander 101
Leslie, David 103
Liberals 141, 153
Lister, Lord 146
Llywelyn 46, 47
Londonderry 106
Luftwaffe 166

McAdam, John 127, 128

Macbeth, King 25
MacDonald, Ramsay 152, 154, 170
Macdonald, Clan 106
Maclean, Hector 67
Magdalen College 76
Maginot Line 164
Magna Carta 42
Malcolm II 26; III 25; IV 34
Mansfield, Lord 131
Margaret of England 71, 76; of Scotland 31
Marlowe, Christopher 96
Marne, battle of 156
Marston Moor, battle of 103
Martyrs, Catholic 82, 85; Protestant 81, 85, 88
Mary I 84; II 105; Queen of Scots 88
Matilda, Empress 31
Maude, Sir Stanley 157
Mayflower 107
Mercia 21
Mersey-Trent Canal 129
Merton College 49
Mesopotamia 157
Metcalfe, Blind Jack 127
Methodists 130, 131
Minden, battle of 116
Monasteries, Dissolution of 82, 83
Mons, retreat from 155
Montfort, Simon de 44, 45
Montgomery, Lord 168
Montrose, Marquis of 101, 103, 104
More, Sir Thomas 82
Moseley, Henry 160
Mosul oilfield 154
Munich conference 165
Mussolini 164
Mystery Plays 95

Napoleon I 133, 134, 135; III 147
Naseby, battle of 103
Nazis 164
Nelson, Admiral 133
Neville, Richard Earl of Warwick 70, 71
Newcomen, Thomas 124, 125
New England 107
Newfoundland 73
Newton, Sir Isaac 27
Newton, Rev John 132
New York 107
Nonconformists 85, 143
Norfolk Four-Course 123
Norman Conquest 27
Nova Scotia 73
Nutmeg 109

Observatory, Royal 112
Oglethorpe, General 130
Osborne Case 153

Palmerston, Lord 147
Park, Mungo 148
Parish Councils 141
Parliament, beginnings of 44; reform of 137, 138, 139, 140
Passchendaele 158
Paterson, William 108
Peasants' Revolt 57
Peel, Sir Robert 136
Penicillin 160
Penn, William 107
Pennsylvania 107
Pepys, Samuel 105
Pétain, Marshal 156
Philip II of Spain 84, 94, 95
Picts 25
Pilgrimage of Grace 83
Pitt, the Elder 116; the Younger 92, 116, 136
Plague of London 110, 112
Poitiers, battle of 56
Poland 165, 166, 168
Porteous, Captain 120
Potwallopers 136
Prayer, Book of Common 84
Pretender, the Old 115, 119; the Young 115
Priestley, Joseph 127
Princes in the Tower 72
Printing 74
Punch 140
Puritans 85, 170
Pym, John 101

Quakers 105, 131, 144
Quebec 116

Radar 166
Radicals 137
Raffles, Sir Stamford 147
Railway legislation 138, 139
Raleigh, Sir Walter 94, 106, 172
Reformation, in England 79, 80, 81, 82, 83; in Scotland 87, 88, 89, 90, 91
Reith, Lord 172
Revolution, English 102; French 116
Rhodes, Cecil 148
Richard I 35, 37; II 58, 59, 96; III 72
Rifles 148
Robert II 55; III 66
Roberts, Lord 149
Roman Conquest 15
Rommel 167, 168

Rosebery, Lord 141
Roses, Wars of the 69 et seq.
Royal Air Force 166
Royal Flying Corps 156
Royal Society 113
Rutherford, Ernest 160

St Andrews University 69
St Paul's School, for boys 85
Saladin the Kurd 38
Saxons 17
Schools 36, 76, 129, 143, 144, 162, 163
Scone 52
Separatists 85, 107
Shaftesbury, Lord 141
Shakespeare, William 96, 172
Sharp, Granville 131
Shaw, Bernard 152
Simpson, Sir James 146
Sinclair, Sir John 124
Slim, General 169
Smoking 107
Somerset, James 131; Protector 84
Stamford Bridge, battle of 27
Standards, battle of 34
Steam engines 124, 125, 126
Steel 145
Stephen, King 34
Stephenson, George 139
Stirling Bridge, battle of 47
Stonehenge 11
Strafford, Earl of 101
Strike, Right to 153
Stuart Succession 97
Suffragettes 154
Suffragists 154
Swan, Sir Joseph 146
Swein Forkbeard 24, 26

Taff Vale Railway case 153
Tanks 158, 159, 167
Television 161
Telford, Thomas 127
Templars, Knights 37
Tenchebrai, battle of 35
Theatre, Elizabethan 96
The Times 149
Thomas, S. C. 145
Tobacco 106
Tompion, Thomas 112
Tonypandy 154
Townshend, Lord 123
Trade Union Amendment Act 1913 153
Trafalgar, battle of 133
Trains, Parliamentary 140
Turnpikes 127

Tyler, Wat 58
Tyndale, William 80

Ulster 99, 154
Union of England and Scotland 99, 117, 118, 119
United States of America 116, 157, 164
Utrecht, Peace of 115

Versailles, Treaty of 164
Victoria, Queen 143, 150
Vikings 22, 23, 24, 25, 26
Virginia 106

Wade, General 119
Wakefield, battle of 71
Wakefield, Edward Gibbon 147
Wales, Statute of 47; Education in 171
Wallace, William 47
Walmer Castle 92
Waterloo, battle of 135
Watt, James 126
Watt, Sir Robert Watson 166
Wavell, General 167
Waynflete, William 76
Wedmore, Treaty of 23
Wellington, Duke of 135, 136, 146
Wells, H. G. 152
Wesley, John 130
Westminster Abbey 27, 30, 49, 50, 77; Hall 27, 61; School 86, 110
Whigs 105
Whitehall, Palace of 101
Wilberforce, William 132, 136
William the Conqueror 27, 28; II 33; III 105, 114, 117; IV 133; the Lion 34, 42
Wilson, President Woodrow 157, 163
Winchester College 62
Wine, Bordeaux 56
Winthrop, John 107
Wishart, George 88
Wolfe, General James 116
Wolsey, Cardinal 80, 81
Wool Trade 57
Wren, Sir Christopher 110, 111, 112
Wyatt, Sir Thomas 84
Wyclif, John 62
Wykeham, William of 62

Xenopsylla cheopis 112

Yarrow boilers 145, 146
Yevele, Henry 61
York, House of 95
Young, Arthur 124

Zionism 157

176